WAR WAGED
—— with ——
KISSES

Negotiation and Mediation for Realists

CHARLES PARSELLE

For information about this title or to order books and/or electronic media, contact the publisher:

Stroud House Publishing

Offices in New York and Anaheim, California

StroudHousePublishing.com

Contact@StroudHousePublishing.com

ISBNs: 978-0-9961335-8-6 (Print)

ISBNs: 978-0-9961335-9-3 (eBooks)

Printed in the United States of America

CONTENTS

INTRODUCTION

If a stranger taps you on the shoulder and requests several hours of your close attention, very likely you will want to know why. Today we never seem to have enough hours. We are rich in stuff but poor in time. So why read a book, which takes scarce hours, mental energy, and eyestrain? Book lovers often describe their books as friends but that comes later, after the effort required reading it.

Every book needs an excuse, an explanation for its existence, some kind of justification for demanding several hours of your time and mental effort. An introduction is the author's attempt to provide a convincing justification.

This book would like to guarantee to repay your investment, but realistically who can guarantee how a relationship will work out? A book may engage one reader but repel another. Style matters as much as content. This book is the product of some thousands of hours practicing and teaching the subject matter by the author.

The topic is human relationships under stress, which is another description of negotiation. Negotiation is certainly stressful, but the stress is very much reduced if one is well prepared. Preparation is a learned skill, but the main preparation is nearly always internal, with oneself. Even so, the more one learns about the dynamics of negotiation, the easier it becomes.

This book is also about mediation, which is assisted negotiation. Some people read books like this wanting to learn tricks and tips that promise victory in every encounter. They want to get a good deal, but also to feel good about themselves. People like bargains, but a negotiation is also a limited, defined relationship with another person, often a stranger. That relationship is intended to reach a conclusion—the deal—but often also produces a winner and a loser. Everyone wants a good deal, but many want to triumph over the other party as well. This complicates matters.

There is a large difference between working towards a "win-win" result, and working to win by producing a loser. Tricks and tips sometimes work but are not a substitute for knowing the principles of effective negotiation. Tricks and tips in this book come with a warning label: use with caution. The subject matter is far broader than tricks and tips, and is intended to provide a great deal of detailed information in a concise and if possible entertaining format.

The first duty of a book is to be readable, so that the reader can proceed from sentence to sentence, paragraph to paragraph, without a sense of undue effort but on the contrary, with a sense of satisfaction and progress being made, with neither omissions of needed material nor unnecessary repetition.

Secondly, a work of non-fiction must provide information that is actually useful to the reader, which can form part of the reader's mental architecture and so provide a permanent basis to assist their understanding.

A book that can satisfy these two requirements is indeed worth its price, both as to the financial cost and more importantly, the time and effort spent in reading it. Although individual books are not usually expensive, many readers have a great many books on their shelves so the expense adds up, even so today's cost of buying a book is usually less than the cost of going out to dinner. In earlier times, it was prohibitively expensive to produce a book, even after the invention of the printing press, and books were daunting to write, considering that until quite recently the writer was obliged to use an archaic instrument like the quill pen.

A glance at the table of contents will provide a good idea of the particular topics. The author taught negotiation and mediation for many years by way of courses that attempted to be comprehensive. The text contains many quotations from different sources and particularly from Shakespeare, not required for an understanding of the subject matter, but with the hope they may provide some enjoyment and illumination.

This book is intended to illustrate the complex dynamics that arise when people negotiate with each other for their own or mutual advantage. It is one thing to have a catchy title, but quite another to understand just how people interact with each other when they are engaged in War Waged With Kisses. It is helpful, indeed necessary, to understand the close relationship between the war and the kisses; or as Winston Churchill once put it, between "war war" and "jaw jaw."

ONE

WHAT ARE YOU WILLING TO DIE FOR

"**W**ar waged with kisses" is a description of negotiation dating back to Saint Augustine of Hippo in the 5th century A.D. Augustine was a ruthless negotiator according to some of the heretics whom he sought to convert. One of them described his negotiating style as "war waged with kisses." He developed the idea of a "just war." He wrote: "We do not seek peace in order to be at war, but we go to war that we may have peace."

Failed negotiations may sometimes lead to war, though not inevitably because sometimes one can just walk away. One can also get disastrously stuck, as King Macbeth discovered to his dismay. "I am in blood stepped in so far, that should I wade no more, returning were as tedious as go o'er." (Shakespeare – Macbeth) The question always is: if we cannot get a settlement, then what is the alternative? Hugs and kisses have their place, but they are not a substitute for realism. Paramount for a negotiator is clear-eyed understanding of what is at risk and what can realistically be achieved. The road to failure is paved with wishful thinking, just as the road to hell is supposedly paved with good intentions.

The limits of negotiation are illustrated by the question: what you are willing to die for? If you are not willing to die for it, then it has a price and can be negotiated. If you are willing to die for it, then it is priceless and cannot be negotiated. In economics, everything has a price and therefore a mathematic quantity, a number. It has to be quantifiable because otherwise it cannot be modeled or programed. "What you are willing to die for?" cannot be modeled or programed, because there are no algorithms for what is, in effect, infinite.

"A cynic is a man who knows the price of everything and the value of nothing," wrote Oscar Wilde. Some reflection is likely to yield the insight that none of the most important things in life are capable of negotiation because they are priceless; such a list is likely to include your children's health, their lives, your liberty and so on, probably a long list of non-negotiables.

Even so, the areas of life amenable to negotiation are extensive. For some people, everything is negotiable, such as famous 19th century robber baron, "Diamond Jim" Fisk, known to posterity for exiting a New York courtroom with the words: "Don't worry, boys. Nothing's lost, save honor," proving that for him honor was not a willing-to-die-for item. Not long after, Fisk was shot dead by his girlfriend's other lover, proving that for the shooter the affection of the lady was non-negotiable. Shakespeare's Henry V claimed to value his honor more highly than gold, quite the reverse of Diamond Jim: "By Jove I am not covetous for gold...but if it be a sin to covet honor, I am the most offending soul alive." (Henry V, Act 4, Scene 3)

NEGOTIATING WITH ONESELF

Anyone who observes negotiation soon learns an odd fact—many people spend much of their time negotiating with themselves. Even when two people are negotiating with each other, each person spends more time negotiating with himself or herself than with the person across the table. Much of any negotiation is internal. Negotiating with oneself is the way in which a person sorts out her mixed, and sometimes conflicting, motivations.

A negotiation is an engagement with uncertainty. Many people are not comfortable with uncertainty and prefer to avoid it. Often they succeed because not all circumstances require negotiation. In most stores including online retailers, the prices are fixed. All you have to do is choose what you want to and pay the advertised price, or walk away. When the clerk at the checkout counter rings up your selection of groceries, if you then say: "Ah, that is too much, but I am willing to make you an offer," the clerk will look baffled. Retailers mostly do not negotiate; instead, they post fixed prices and avoid uncertainty.

Some circumstances require negotiation. All such circumstances contain uncertainty.

Uncertainly demands negotiation. Negotiation is what you must do when you want something and the price is not fixed. Negotiating in those circumstances is called bargaining, and everyone likes to get a good bargain, and even more so wants to avoid a bad deal. A person who wants a good bargain is equally worried that she might get taken advantage of. People like to boast about the bargains they have just acquired. They are more apt to say "I got a fabulous bargain," than they are to boast about the item itself. A person's self-esteem is bound up with getting a bargain. This applies in the most trivial of circumstances as well as the relationships between nations.

Some relationships are ongoing and require ongoing negotiation. Some relationships are limited to the business at hand, after which the parties will never see each other again. The way negotiations are conducted partly depends on the nature of the relationship between the parties.

The better prepared is the negotiator, the less time she will spend negotiating, or agonizing, with herself during the negotiation. Sometimes negotiators hire a mediator to help them with the conduct of the negotiation. The mediator's job is to help the negotiating parties get through the stressful process of negotiation to their mutual satisfaction.

MEDIATION

Mediation is a process in which an impartial person helps the disputing participants define, understand, and resolve their dispute. It is voluntary, collaborative, and confidential. Mediation is built on a triple foundation of Etiquette, Ethics, and Aesthetics, corresponding to the rules of behavior, the discipline of right conduct, and the art of achieving results with elegance and panache.

ETIQUETTE

Etiquette is the discipline of behavior. It consists of the appropriate ways of behaving in a given circumstance. Etiquette is the subject of how to go along in order to get along. Etiquette is the study of behavior. The reason there are books on etiquette that explain the rules of how to hold a knife and fork, or what to wear on a given occasion, or how to begin and end a letter, is because such rules of social intercourse are important to know and can be disastrous not to know. The person who does not know the rules is likely to feel ill at ease and will appear gauche to others; this inhibits the smooth interaction that makes discourse and cooperation possible among human beings. It has a formal aspect yet is a bridge to intimacy.

The mediator is called upon to deal with different kinds of people who often have their own ideas of how to behave in a given circumstance. The mediator must be able to deal easily and comfortably with these varied individuals, and to do this, it is helpful, indeed necessary, to know the etiquette of mediation.

Invariably when individuals and groups come to a mediator for assistance they will thankfully yield to the mediator's idea of proper etiquette, provided the mediator knows the etiquette of her own subject and is willing to convey it to those in front of her. Having a general pattern in which to operate, and having mastered numerous little guides that work well in a variety of situations, the mediator can both possess and instill in others a sense of confidence that holds their uncertainty in check. As the mediation progresses, the mediator's calm demeanor influences the parties toward a rational outcome. This is the etiquette of the subject.

ETHICS

Ethics is the discipline of right conduct. The mediator must learn to act ethically within the terms of the discipline that is mediation.

Ethics is often presented as a subject of black and white, that is to say, as if a particular act or action was either right or wrong, but it is rarely as simple as that. More often one finds that certain actions are more right or more wrong without being absolutely one way or the other. Most actions are complex and nuanced, and rather than finding ourselves in a world of black and white, we are more likely to find a world that is predominantly gray, in which it is not easy to weigh the consequences, desirability, or principled consideration of a particular course of action.

Although we talk about etiquette as proper behavior and ethics also as proper behavior or action, in practice the rules of ethics always refer to a set of guiding principles, often embedded in appeals to higher authority (e.g., the Ten Commandments), whereas the rules of etiquette are practical and generally without an outside reference source. The rules of etiquette are designed to make us and others feel comfortable, but the rules of ethics arise out of more complex considerations.

For a mediator the formal ethical rules of the subject are quite simple but do not afford a great deal of guidance in the intimate situation of the mediation room. It is easy, for example, for a mediator to understand that she should be impartial, but how precisely is the principle of impartiality to be applied? The mediator may find it necessary to spend an hour with one person but only fifteen minutes with the other. She would be in error to suppose that impartiality means that every person in the room must be allowed to utter precisely the same number of words. The mediator must remain "neutral" as to outcome but not necessarily "impartial" in her views of the merits.

One side may be more realistic and the other more illusory about the situation. The mediator needs to be able to notice the distinction and not treat these two as if they were the same. Impartiality is an overarching principle governing the attitude of the mediator toward her work, but as things progress minute by minute the mediator will very often find herself now on one side and now on the other; her job is to help the parties reach accommodation based on a realistic assessment of what is going on between them.

AESTHETICS

Aesthetics is the third pillar on which the subject of mediation rests. It is the most elusive but also most interesting, and distinguishes great mediators from the merely talented. Aesthetics is the study of elegance in achieving the most effective solution in the circumstances. The aesthetic solution is one that leads to the best possible result in the most concise and satisfying manner. Aesthetics encompasses more than art. Some skills in sports take our breath away. We may look on a poem as aesthetically pleasing, thus "make dust our paper and with rainy eyes, write sorrow on the bosom of the earth," but a scientific statement may also be an aesthetic triumph, for example, $E = mc^2$. The deal making that is the subject of mediation may also be done with such concision and elegance that it makes the heart sing.

WAR IS THE FORCE THAT GIVES US MEANING?

At one level, disputants tend to cherish their disputes and the emotions and attitudes that accompany them; there is something in it for them. At another level, they want to lay down the burden. They want the satisfaction that accompanies winning but are afraid of losing. Some also want not merely to win but the other side to lose, and preferably be seen to lose. Only when the burden of a dispute outweighs the perceived benefits are disputants likely to seek a mediator to help them resolve it.

When an outsider hears both sides of a conflict, she may get the impression that the disputants are living in illusion, with their competing illusions colliding in conflict. One or both of them has got it wrong; each side estimates it has a better than 50% chance of winning. If both sides are brought to share roughly the same perception of the dispute, they generally settle. To accomplish this, each must learn the ability to see the dispute through the other's eyes. This comes across in various colloquial expressions such as "the same ballpark," "the same postal code," or "the zone of possible agreement." The presence and skills of the mediator tilt the balance in favor of reality, rationality, and closure.

Because conflicts come to mediation in a state of impasse, some change is needed for movement to occur. Movement is needed for the disputants to approach each other. The disputants must approach each other for negotiation to occur. Negotiation must occur for solutions to be explored. Solutions must be explored for the disputants to achieve a resolution that satisfies competing interests.

"War Is The Force That Gives Us Meaning" (Chris Hedges, 2014)

TWO

WHAT WE TALK ABOUT WHEN WE TALK ABOUT MEDIATION

Mediation assumes that parties attend mediation to negotiate in good faith. In practice, however, the mediator may be dismayed to realize that parties might spend a good deal of money attending mediation without actually negotiating. It may also be startling to discover that someone's idea of negotiation is the other side's absolute surrender, and when both sides think this way, the mediator has a job on her hands.

The initial task of a mediator may be to bring the parties to the point at which they will commence negotiating. The mediator must accomplish this without resorting to coercion; thumbscrews are disapproved, and hanging is out of the question. Once the parties begin negotiating in earnest, chances are high that they will actually settle. It may take them a while to settle down, and sometimes they may not get to the point of being willing to negotiate until the second or third mediation session.

Example: a serious vehicle accident left the driver quadriplegic. Very high-powered lawyers attend a very expensive mediation; they have reserved a whole day. But do they mediate? No, they do not. The plaintiff demands $25 million. The defendants offer $1 million. The plaintiff promptly lowers the demand to $20 million, which is too large a move in too short a time.

The defendant responds by raising its offer to $1,050,000, a move so trivial as to constitute no move at all. The plaintiff responds by walking out. This is not negotiating; it is more like a child on a beach running toward the water, putting a toe in, and running back.

The predominant emotion of parties who attend mediation, including in many instances the attorneys, is low-intensity fear, which may best be described as apprehension or nervousness. This is the emotion of fear, expressed in low volume. The energy of the emotion of fear is characterized by the desire to leave. However, it is necessary that parties to mediation stay there long enough to accomplish something.

BE PRESENT, BE ATTENTIVE, BE OF SERVICE

If your entire training consisted of only three rules, these would be they, and if you knew and practiced them, you would be a very effective person. The golden rules are: be present, be attentive, and be of service.

Groucho Marx (among others) is credited with saying, "Eighty percent of success is showing up." This may seem obvious, yet some people seem to think that there are only two obligatory attendances in one's life—birth and death—and that showing up for everything in between is optional. A mediator has to show up and stay present.

There are variations. One can show up late, unprepared, unfocused, biased, or prejudiced. It is not really enough to drag one's body into the room and slump into a chair; one must bring certain qualities and attributes. The most important of these is attention, for which there is no substitute. Full attention is probably the most valuable thing a mediator can give to participants. If you sit opposite and give someone your full attention, she is apt to open up and start communicating. How many mediators walk into a room and give a ten- or fifteen-minute speech? There are not too many who can get away with speaking for half an hour, but there are some. Probably a one-minute speech is enough. Many highly regarded mediators do not start with any speech at all. Their focus is on getting the parties to communicate. The role of the mediator is to use her skills to carry the conversation forward.

It is possible, and many people try, to fake attention, and perhaps this is so prevalent because many of us learned to fake paying attention during our schooldays so that we were able to sit at our desks with our eyes open looking absorbed. Many professionals practice that habit, but faking attention works only for a short time. At some level speakers really do get it when the listener is faking attention, but they also get it and appreciate it when the mediator is truly listening.

The second rule—be attentive—has likewise been around for a long time. As the legendary comedian George Burns put it, "In show business sincerity is everything, and if you can fake that you've got it made." The laugh lies in the oxymoron, and the same applies to authenticity. Authenticity in mediation may perhaps be achieved by being genuinely attentive. One may not know if one is being "authentic," but one certainly knows if one is paying attention.

The third rule is to be of service. Although authenticity is not an easy concept to define, much less put into practice, one can achieve great results by learning to be of service. That means working on behalf of the people who have come for help in resolving their dispute.

The three rules build one on the other. You cannot get anything done unless you actually show up. You have to be attentive to find out what is going on. Only then can you determine what is necessary in order for you to be of service. You show up, you pay attention to the situation, and you determine how to be of service.

The participants are there because they need a service from you, and it is not enough to say that the service you are providing is mediation. That is way too general. In each situation there are specific ways in which you can be of service to help those participants meet their objectives. Of course, it is true that the objectives of different participants do not coincide. If they coincided there would be no dispute and no need for your presence and assistance. But at least one of the objectives of the participants is to achieve closure of their dispute. A party's objective is not a single thing but usually a bundle of aims that each would like to achieve. By helping the parties sort out their own desires and prioritize them, and by helping them see the situation clearly, the mediator becomes of service to both sides and the dispute gets resolved.

COMPETITION AND COOPERATION

There are two modes of existing in the world with other people. The first is competition, and the second is cooperation. Parties come to mediation in competition, but they need to engage in cooperation. This is the mediator's job. Cooperation is harder than competition, and in many cases people will not cooperate with each other unless they believe they have no better option. The reason for this is that cooperation requires engagement and, when people are nervous or apprehensive about each other, the tendency is for them to separate, whereas in order to cooperate it is necessary to approach and engage.

People come to mediation because they have come to the conclusion that a form of cooperation is more likely to be an improvement for them than continued competition. This is because competition can be expensive; it is also risky. Therefore, parties arrive at mediation with expressed or unexpressed reluctance, and they are likely to spend a certain amount of time—sometimes quite a lot of time—explaining to the mediator, in a roundabout way, why they are not willing to move from the position they held when they arrived and expressing the strong hope that the mediator will be able to get the other side to move.

Consider a big conflict such as Israel versus Egypt. During many years, there were several wars. That was competition. Finally, the two countries made peace; the peace was brokered—or, as we would say, mediated—by President Carter. That was cooperation. Carter was able to accomplish the Camp David Accords because of the prestige of the United States and the pressure it was able to bring on the warring parties.

LIABILITY AND DAMAGES

In mediating litigated cases, one finds that every case has two components: liability and damages. Both sides will attempt to explain to the mediator why "liability is on our side." In any mediation one side must make a move in order for any kind of negotiation to begin. The problem faced by the mediator is that each side perceives it as weakness to make the first move. Each side is faced with the prisoner's dilemma, which is based on the inability of the two prisoners to trust each other. The task of the mediator is to find a way safely out of the dilemma for both sides so that they can each act in his or her own best interest without fear of betrayal.

FROM POSTURING TO NEGOTIATING

Therefore, the first stage of mediation may be characterized as "not negotiating but posturing." First, the parties will explain to the mediator how their position is absolutely correct and how the other side's position is absolutely incorrect. In many situations, the parties feel emotionally wounded by what has happened; they have been bruised in competition with each other. Perhaps one side has initiated litigation and the other side has been compelled to respond. Both sides have retained attorneys, and the attorneys themselves may have exacerbated each other's feelings. Even though attorneys are trained professionally, and often do not express emotion, there is always some emotion driving them. They posture until they are ready to negotiate.

The primary task of the mediator is to persist and to carefully watch the dynamics of the parties and the attorneys, because during mediation if the mediator is sensitive to it, she will observe a remarkable thing happening. The parties and the attorneys will start to change their positions. This is the huge difference between mediation, on one hand, and trials or arbitration hearings, on the other. Parties may and often do go to trial or to arbitration without ever engaging in meaningful communication with each other. Even during mediation, parties often communicate with each other only through the medium of the mediator. But at the trial level, no party is required to have any change of mind. Each side goes into battle and, as forcefully as possible, pleads their respective positions to the judge or the arbitrator. All communication is from the party to the judge, and from the other party to the judge, and no communication is required to be made between the parties.

Mediation is entirely different. The parties must necessarily engage in communication with each other, however cautious that communication may be, however stilted, with whatever emotion of apprehension or anger or resentment or outrage, and even if all communications are made via the mediator. Even so, as the parties sit in the mediation, either in the same room or very often in separate rooms, their attention is focused on the problem at hand. That is why it is so very important that the parties attend the mediation in person. If the mediator consents to mediation by telephone so that a party is simply on the other end of a telephone line, then they are not really involved in the mediation at all and it is more difficult to effect a resolution.

After an indeterminate length of time, the mediator may sense a shift in the momentum of the room. The first part of the mediation often feels to the mediator as if she is pushing a heavy weight up a hill. That is the weight of the party's emotion, which may be an emotion of apprehension or an impulse, suppressed or not, to run away or to be somewhere else. But eventually the concentrated attention on the subject at hand by the parties is likely to lead to a kind of realization that they are going to need to move if the matter is to be resolved. Then there is a shift in the energy in the room, and at that time it will be possible for true negotiation to begin.

Any negotiation proceeds by way of offers and counteroffers. In a legal setting, the plaintiff is said to make a "demand" and the defendant is said to make an "offer" or "counteroffer." The negotiation proceeds by way of demands and counteroffers until agreement is reached.

THE ZONE OF POSSIBLE AGREEMENT - ZOPA

Some people divide the stages through which demands and/or offers proceed as a series of zones—for example, an insult zone, a credible zone, a reasonable zone, a zone of possible agreement.

The insult zone is a demand that bears no conceivable rational relationship to the value of the matter being negotiated. Likewise, an insult counteroffer is exactly what the name suggests—an offer that is likely to be perceived by the other side as insulting to its intelligence. The exchange of insults is simply an indication that the parties have not reached the point at which they are ready to get serious about negotiation.

The second stage may be called the credible zone—an offer that is nowhere near the zone of possible agreement but is not so far out of line as to be perceived as incredible or insulting. Once a party makes an offer that may be perceived by the other side as being reasonable, though not acceptable, there will be a shift in the dynamics of energy in the room and real negotiation may begin.

Finally, the parties should reach the zone of possible agreement—ZOPA—which may be defined as the zone in which the demand is within the range of acceptability and the offer is within the range of acceptability. In other words, it has taken the time that it has taken for the parties to reach the range in which the case should settle.

COMPETING ILLUSIONS

Negotiation usually commences with competing illusions. Those illusions are in collision, and the mediator may become confused on hearing the stories of each side to realize that they do not seem to bear much resemblance. The job of a mediator is to separate fact from fancy, reconcile conflicting facts, and coax the parties into the realm of reality, which is the ZOPA. The zone of possible agreement is the range in which the true value of the case is to be found, and the value of the case may be anywhere within that zone of possible agreement.

The mediator cannot do this all by herself, but fortunately she does not have to. The powerful force working on the side of the mediator is the parties' own attention and brainpower. Working against the mediator are the parties' negative emotions and reactivity, their tendency both to run from the problem yet cling to it. This is sometimes expressed in actually leaving the mediation, but another manifestation of it is anger, which is an expression of the desire to do battle and not negotiate. Battle is competitive; negotiation is cooperative. These are the two fundamental different modes in which human beings interact.

Over the next generation, I predict, society's greatest opportunities will lie in tapping human inclinations toward collaboration and compromise rather than stirring our proclivities for competition and rivalry. [These may be] the most creative social experiments of our time.

—Derek Bok,
(former) president of Harvard University

Such "tapping human inclinations" toward collaboration and compromise is what mediators attempt. It should be easy, but it is not. The reason it is not easy is because of negative emotion and reactivity.

How do conflicts arise? There is a primary reason. When two creatures seek to occupy the same space or possess the same object, they collide in conflict. This is true of the animal kingdom as well. Prey animals fight over the possession of territory and over the possession of females. Grazing animals do not fight over territory as they inhabit the same territory in herds, but males fight over the opportunity to impregnate a female. Some animals compete for food. Conflict arises over competition for space or objects.

Humans also collide in competition for territory or possessions, but having memory and foresight complicates their disputes. Envy, jealousy, pride, rage, spite, despair, apathy, terror, pain, and desire for revenge are all subject to arousal in a human on the losing side of a conflict that was originally over occupying territory or possession of an object. When two animals have fought and one has lost, that is the end of the matter. There are no blood feuds among animals. But humans in conflict often forget what they were fighting about, and instead the object of the fight becomes about defeating the other side; in other words, conflicts become about emotional satisfaction, and the emotions sought to be satisfied are always negative ones.

A good deal of human conflict is derivative. The original reason for the conflict sometimes disappears altogether, but the parties fight on, trying by external means to heal their internal wounds. The function of the mediator is to help them shed these debilitating burdens and free them to devote their energies to life rather than to a conflict that has become sterile and self-punishing.

EVALUATIVE MEDIATION

An evaluative mediator is prepared to express an opinion as to the likely outcome of a dispute. Parties who seek an evaluative mediator will often choose a person in authority whose judgment they respect. The prerequisite for giving an evaluation is subject matter expertise. Judges, who have adjudicated many cases and observed numerous juries reaching verdicts, are often trusted by parties to render an evaluation, which the parties may find useful in coming to their own decision about their particular dispute. Lawyers as well as retired judges are used for the purpose of evaluation.

Persons engaged in a construction dispute will often go to an engineer, general contractor, or other person with subject matter expertise. In indigenous societies, the headman may be called in to give advice and lend his authority to the process of reconciliation. In international conflicts, a respected leader of another country may be called upon to intervene. This happened when U.S. President Jimmy Carter mediated successfully between the leaders of Israel and Egypt—the so-called Camp David accords. In an evaluative mediation, the perceived authority of the mediator is relied upon by participants to lend credibility to an agreement, even though the decision to settle, and on what terms, remains with the participants. Parties may prefer an evaluative mediator when they wish to resolve their dispute and proceed their separate ways.

FACILITATIVE MEDIATION

A facilitative mediator stresses that the function of her job is to enable, or facilitate, parties to communicate and negotiate with each other in order to arrive at their own evaluation and resolution. She is focused on the process and unwilling to attempt to persuade a particular outcome. A facilitative mediator may consider it unethical to render an opinion. The facilitative style may require great patience and skill in enabling parties to craft their own resolution, whereas an evaluative mediator is more likely to want to "cut to the chase." Facilitative mediation may be more desirable when the parties wish to, or must, engage in a continuing relationship with each other and view the particular dispute as merely a roadblock that needs to be overcome in order to enable that continuing relationship.

Many mediators are perfectly willing to be either evaluative or facilitative, as the situation demands. A mediator may start with facilitation and proceed toward evaluation as she learns more of the dispute and the participants learn to trust her.

TRANSFORMATIVE MEDIATION

The third type of mediator is called transformative, and the goal of transformative mediation is bolder, and more like therapy, than the goal of evaluative or facilitative mediation. This type suggests that the goal of mediation is to effect a transformation, within the parties themselves and in their relationship with each other.

In *Mediating Dangerously*, Kenneth Cloke, a pioneer of transformational mediation, explains:

> The transformational…model of mediation… views conflict as something to be learned from, and the parties as ready for introspection and fundamental change. The mediator becomes an empathetic yet honest agent, whose role is to elicit recognition and empower the parties to solve their own problems. Whether evaluative, facilitative, or transformative, the function of a mediator is to enable change. A mediator is a catalyst whose presence and skills enable change. The type of change so enabled is often the most difficult of all—change of mind.

THREE

OTHER FORMS OF DISPUTE RESOLUTION

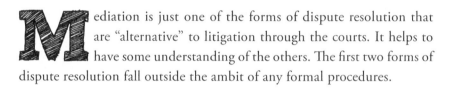ediation is just one of the forms of dispute resolution that are "alternative" to litigation through the courts. It helps to have some understanding of the others. The first two forms of dispute resolution fall outside the ambit of any formal procedures.

AVOIDANCE

Avoidance is a consciously chosen strategy in response to a perceived conflict. This strategy may be called "Get out of Dodge City." There is nothing wrong with getting out of Dodge City in the face of a stronger opponent, a prize not worth fighting for, fear of worse, or any other number of motivations. People routinely, and often sensibly, respond to provocation by just ignoring it.

SELF HELP

Self-help lies at the other end of the scale of extrajudicial processes. Self-help is an action taken by a person designed to affect a resolution of a problem. Self-help includes murder, though not all forms of self-help are illegal. There are potentially debilitating consequences to murder. Blood feuds may last for generations and infect an entire society. Other forms of less drastic self-help may include protesting, striking, and theft. Both avoidance and self-help are unilateral and unorganized. All other forms are more or less organized and are bilateral or multilateral.

NEGOTIATION

Straddling the border between organized and unorganized systems is negotiation. Negotiation is by far the most common method used in all societies for resolving disputes. Most negotiations take place outside any formal procedure. Indeed, people engage in negotiations constantly, on a daily basis, as they navigate their way through the day. When a conflict becomes serious enough to involve other people, it moves from the unorganized into the organized area of dispute resolution, and many people retain attorneys or other negotiators to do their negotiating on their behalf.

If negotiations prove unfruitful in terms of affecting resolution, then the parties may simply walk away from the deal. If they cannot, they may resort to arbitration, which is an acknowledged form of alternative dispute resolution and is very often given legal sanction, meaning that arbitration awards can be enforced in a court of law.

Of all methods of conflict resolution, only negotiation requires that the disputants talk to each other, even if they choose to do so through a mediator. All other methods of conflict resolution are essentially unilateral, and their common liability is that conflicts handled unilaterally are not really resolved at all. In searching for justice, one often finds her in the company of her ugly little sister; her name is Revenge.

ARBITRATION

In arbitration, the parties have made the decision that they wish to avoid two features of a court trial. The first is the great expense of litigation; the second is the public nature of litigation. Arbitration is private, and the decision reached by an arbitrator is between the parties to that arbitration only. Generally speaking, arbitration is much cheaper than a fully litigated case. Parties to arbitration also have the luxury of choosing an arbitrator rather than accepting whichever judge the court system provides them. Also, in a litigated case all parties must conform to the schedule laid down by the court, and the court's system consults the convenience of judges more than the convenience of the parties, whereas in an arbitration the parties can adjust the schedule with the arbitrator according to their own needs and preferences.

However, arbitration shares with the court system one critical feature. The parties to arbitration are not free to craft their own solution to the problem. Instead, they have already agreed that the decision of the arbitrator will be binding upon all parties. In this sense, arbitration is the same as a trial by judge or jury, which also contains the feature that the parties are bound by the decision and that decision will generally result in a winner and a loser.

The great majority of arbitrations are contractual, coming about by reason of a prior agreement between the parties to permit a third person, the arbitrator, to decide the issue between them. The courts are supportive of contractual agreements to arbitration, and the courts will generally uphold arbitration awards. When the parties choose an arbitrator to make the decision for them, they risk that the decisions of arbitrators are, in nearly all cases, not subject to any appeal.

The arbitrator's decision is final, even if the arbitrator "got the facts wrong" and even if the arbitrator made a mistake in law. The grounds upon which an arbitrator's award can be challenged are usually very limited, relating to proven corruption, undisclosed conflict of interest, or excess of jurisdiction, on the part of the arbitrator. In this sense, an arbitrator has more absolute power than a judge or jury, whose decisions are subject potentially to two levels of appeal.

It does not hurt to be reminded that the court system itself was once an alternative dispute resolution process and has superseded older forms of dispute resolution, some of which are trial by battle, trial by ordeal, trial by compurgation, and trial by torture.

TRIAL BY BATTLE

People used to believe that in the event of a dispute, the disputants should resolve the issue by battling it out between themselves, and indeed this method still prevails today: Western movies are full of such examples. In addition to the strategy of avoidance ("Get out of Dodge City"), there is the strategy of confrontation (*Gunfight at the O.K. Coral, High Noon*).

This procedure was formalized in the early middle ages when it became the custom for a disputant to pick a champion to engage in the battle on his behalf. It was still the case that the winner of the battle also won the argument, but the individual disputant did not have to risk his own neck in order to achieve this kind of "justice." Knights in medieval times would engage in tournaments, at which they would start at one end of the run and proceed at full tilt on horseback toward their opponent, also on horseback and wearing heavy armor. The lances would strike the galloping bodies, and if each survived that encounter they would gallop to the other end of the run and turn in order to face the opposite direction and start again. This turning point was called the tourney, and the knight was said to be "at the tourney," or "a tourney," from which we derive the modern term *attorney*.

TRIAL BY ORDEAL

Trial by ordeal could be called an unfairly weighted system, often used to "try" witches. The unfortunate lady would be weighed down with stones in a sack and thrown into a pond. If she survived, that was by the grace of God and she was innocent. If she drowned (nearly always the case), that proved she was guilty. She might be made to grasp burning coals; if by God's mercy her hand did not blister, she was innocent. It may readily be seen that this kind of "trial" was used in instances where the allegation was impossible to prove, and women were the likely sufferers.

TRIAL BY COMPURGATION

Trial by compurgation was an ancient system whereby a disputant would bring forward friends to swear an oath on his behalf that his story was correct. This primitive method of resolving a dispute relied upon the not unsophisticated proposition, in an Age of Faith, that where a person had sworn an oath on the Bible to tell the truth, she would be risking his soul to damnation if she lied. But it appeared that many people were prepared to take that risk in order to help a friend.

COLLABORATIVE LAW

Collaborative law is a fairly new system, well suited to marital dissolution cases. The parties and their lawyers make an agreement in advance to work out the terms of the divorce collaboratively rather than competitively, meaning without using the abrasive and costly procedures of litigation. What if they cannot? The agreement requires that if agreement is not attained, then the parties may proceed with litigation but must obtain new attorneys to do so. If the lawyers fail to reach agreement, they are off the case. If the parties must retain new attorneys, it greatly increases costs. Both parties and attorneys thus have strong incentive to reach agreement and, more than that, merely making the collaborative agreement in the first place reduces the tension and stress that accompanies the breakup of a marriage. Especially when children are involved, a workable continuing relationship between the parents is greatly enhanced by a collaborative process and so often greatly impaired by the traditional adversarial process.

RETRIBUTIVE JUSTICE VS. RESTORATIVE JUSTICE

Retributive justice asks three questions: What rule has been broken? Who is to blame? How do we make the wrongdoer pay?

Restorative justice asks three different questions: Who has been hurt? What are that person's needs? Who is obligated to address those needs?

MEDIATION

Mediation asks, "How can we bring these disputants together in a meaningful exchange that will permit them to end the conflict in a mutually satisfactory manner and, in appropriate instances, achieve reconciliation?"

WRONG TARGET

Sometimes a person picks a fight out of the blue. One is attacked without warning, perhaps mistaken for someone else. One may be attacked at random.

"*Do you really believe there's some stored-up conflict that exists between us? There is no 'us.' It doesn't exist. So if there's someone you want to hit, it isn't me.*"

—Grosse Pointe Blank, movie.

FOUR

RACEHORSES
AND LAWSUITS

Placing a value on lawsuits and racehorses is difficult. Racehorses are riskier, but lawsuits are more complicated because two competing theories of value—the market price and the just price—are implicated in every lawsuit. The theories are not complementary but competitive, and of the two, the concept of a just price has taxed the brightest minds

Market price is simple enough to express; it is what a willing buyer will pay a willing seller, yet the willing buyer and seller are like the reasonable man: they exist only as abstractions. The buyer may be desperate, the seller predatory; the market doesn't care. The price of the transaction is always exactly right, in retrospect (ex post facto); the theory fulfills itself even though it cannot predict the result in advance. In the practice of law, we deal with market prices every day. In both state and federal courts, more than 95 percent of cases settle, and every time a case settles out of court, it settles for the price a "willing" buyer is prepared to pay a "willing" seller. The concept of market price is the foundation of capitalism, and capitalism finds its way into the legal system at every turn.

In economic theory, one talks of the exchange of "goods." Anything that can be exchanged is a good, even if the item exchanged is not what we would ordinarily describe by the adjective *good*. For example, pollution is an exchangeable commodity, a good. In the commercial world, transactions occur in the present and relate to the future, but in lawsuits, one half of the transaction has already taken place; to express it in the language of economics, the defendant has allegedly received a good from the plaintiff, but the plaintiff has not been paid. In the language of law, however, we do not say that the defendant has received something good without paying for it; we say the plaintiff has received something bad without being compensated for it. Here we can speak of a willing buyer and a willing seller only in the most attenuated sense.

The language of the law is not the same as the language of economics. Instead of claiming that the defendant has received something of value, the plaintiff alleges that she has been "wronged." The language of fault is imposed on the concept of exchange. The plaintiff claims to have lost something of value, for example, her health, her business, or the roof of her house, for which the other party to the event or transaction failed to pay the price. The defendant must be made to pay the price. But what is the price, when there was an exchange of some kind yet no willing buyer, no willing seller? The elusive concept of the just price survives to provide the answer.

In a capitalist world, the legal system is the last bastion of the other competing theory of value—the just price—and the legal system will always have to deal with the just price, because justice is what the legal system is all about. When a case goes to trial, there is no talk of market price. The willing buyer and willing seller fade away. In their place, the demanding "seller" (plaintiff) and the unwilling "buyer" (defendant) step forward. These parties must present, explain, justify, cajole, plead, and persuade the court why each side's version of "the price" is the "just price."

The theory of the just price has antecedents, ancient and modern, and they make strange bedfellows. Religious and secular authorities in the Middle Ages were intensely interested in establishing criteria for the prices of things. They did not believe that matters would take care of themselves or believe in an "invisible hand" setting prices. How ironic that the thoroughly metaphysical concept of an invisible hand should be left to a quintessential eighteenth-century rationalist, Adam Smith. The medieval scholastics did not believe that prices should be left to whatever the market would bear; they believed, in short, in a price that was "just."

And so did Karl Marx! The great enemy of capitalism devoted much thought to the same enterprise that occupied the intellects of his great enemies, the Churchmen. Marx was equally against capitalism and religion, but both Marx and Christianity struggled mightily to develop theories of pricing that would be just in all circumstances, without success. How ironic that legal practice, while eschewing grand theories, also struggles mightily on a case-by-case basis to arrive at the value that satisfies the demands of justice.

Whereas in trial the concept of the just price dominates the proceeding pretrial, the concept of the willing buyer and willing seller is paramount. In mediated negotiation, one can watch the tension between the just price and the market price as it plays out in the negotiating process. Mediation is the only forum in which this occurs. In the business world, the market rules—anything and everything is exchanged for "what the market will bear." In the courtroom, the market is banished and everything depends on the judge's or jury's view of the just value to be placed on the transaction in dispute.

But mediation always occurs with trial as a potential option; therefore in mediation, attorneys and parties must perform the considerable intellectual feat of negotiating using both the concept of willing buyer/seller and the concept of the just price at the same time. The parties must work with these twin ideas: What will the market bear? What is the just price? Usually, plaintiffs initially talk in terms of justice, the just or correct amount, whereas defendants calculate what the "market" (i.e., the plaintiff) will bear. During the course of the mediation, plaintiffs find themselves moving toward a "market price"—finding themselves obliged to calculate the relative value of the offer now "on the table," compared with how much they would have to win at trial to net the same amount. Both sides have to calculate the costs involved in taking the case to trial. Defendants also use the calculus of the just price, because they have to—they have to because that is how the jury will evaluate the claim if it doesn't settle. Therefore, one sees both sides using a complex mixture of rationales to move from one position to another.

However the parties choose to negotiate, they are always working with these twin ideas—what is fair and just in the circumstances versus what the other side will accept given the stresses and strains of litigation. It is complicated, but in the final analysis, fewer people make money on racehorses.

FIVE
THE SATISFACTIONS OF LITIGATION

In my youth, said the sage, I took to the law
And argued each case with my wife
And the muscular strength it gave to my jaw
Has lasted the rest of my life.

—Lewis Carroll

When we talk about ADR—alternative dispute resolution—we are talking about alternatives to litigation. Litigation is partly what drives mediation. It is also, partly, the competition. Litigation is attractive to people. We need to know why litigation is so attractive. What does litigation offer people?

Litigation is "adversarial." All metaphors to do with litigation are of war, battle, conflict, crushing the enemy, scoring a home run, winning, and—oh yes—losing. Half of those who step into the ring come out a loser. Like tossing a coin, statistically the proportion of winners to losers is exactly 50:50. The winner takes all.

"Winning isn't everything; it's the only thing."

—Vince Lombardi,
American football coach.

Many conflicts are avoided by means of diplomacy. War is what happens when diplomacy fails. Even Hitler didn't send in storm troopers if he could get his way by bluffing. In the nineteenth century, the British used to send a diplomat to do the talking, and a gunboat for emphasis; it was called "gunboat diplomacy." The goals are the same; the methods differ greatly.

"War is a continuation of diplomacy by other means."

—Clausewitz

The alternative to a litigated result is a negotiated result. Negotiation is an alternative to litigation. It is also an alternative to war. Mediation is a facilitated form of negotiation. So when we talk about mediation as a means of alternative dispute resolution, we are contrasting it with litigation. Litigation is the standard method. Litigation is what law students go to law school to learn. The legal system is a vast edifice composed of courtrooms staffed by judges and court personnel, the attorneys who practice before them, the law schools that teach them, and the long tradition that fills the libraries with the endless statutes and decisions that compose "the law." Litigants retain attorneys to plead their cases before the courts. This is the state-sponsored and approved method of resolving disputes in our society. This system has been in place for hundreds of years. It is not likely to go away any time soon.

A great deal of mediation is practiced in the context of the litigated case. To some extent, the legal profession has incorporated mediation into the litigation process, not as an alternative means of resolving the dispute entirely but as a substitute for a court or jury trial. Mediation in this sense has been coopted into the litigation process.

Lawsuits have been described as: "Clumsy, noisy, unwieldy and notoriously inefficient. Fueled by bad feelings, they generate much heat and friction, yet produce little that is of any use. Worst of all, once set in motion, they are well-nigh impossible to bring to a halt."

—Alex Kozinski,
American judge

One may reasonably wonder why people are so ready to avail themselves of lawsuits. What is the basis for the strong public demand for a system that so many legal professionals find so unsatisfactory? What is the attraction when the statistical failure rate is 50 percent? Shakespeare fully understood the attraction of the law. In *The Merchant of Venice*, the merchant Shylock expresses his demands for justice in striking language:

The pound of flesh, which I demand of him,
Is dearly bought, 'tis mine and I will have it.
If you deny me, fie upon your law…
I stand here for the law.

In answer, the lawyer Portia pleads for mercy for her client, indelibly expressing the flaw in our ideas about justice:

Therefore, though justice be thy plea, consider this,
That, in the course of justice, none of us
Should see salvation. We do pray for mercy.

Shylock rejects her argument: "My deeds upon my head! I crave the law." This does not work out at all well for him, as he loses everything. That can happen in litigation.

Justice is about winning and inflicting loss. Mediation is about acceptable results. Justice cannot be about acceptable mutual results, because one side always loses. Justice is not about getting things done in the shortest possible time, as lawsuits are notoriously slow. Mediation can accomplish a satisfactory result within a day. Justice is not about minimum stress; it is about conflict. It is in its nature stressful; it is about undergoing the ordeal.

When people get into a legal dispute, they naturally go to an attorney for advice and help, and attorneys are trained in the adversarial processes of the common law. Just as medical students go to medical school to learn medicine as practiced by the medical profession, and not "fringe" alternative procedures, so law students are taught what the majority of the legal profession is practicing.

One might feel free to wonder, if the adversarial system is so painful, destructive, and inefficient, why do the legislatures and judiciaries of this country not take steps to alter the system so as to make it less painful, less destructive, and more efficient? Perhaps many have the desire to do so but reforms are difficult to achieve.

When a system has been in place for so long, and when all the law schools of the country are devoted to training young people in the intricacies of that very system, and when the livelihoods of every person who works within the system depends upon it, then it is asking a lot to expect that change will come from within. That goes a long way to account for the growth in the alternative dispute resolution system.

Even though the majority of filed cases do not go to trial but are settled, and even though mediation is frequently used in effecting settlement, it is seen as an adjunct to, and not as substitute for, the litigation process. Some cases get dismissed, or otherwise fall by the wayside (somebody dies, the parties cannot afford to continue, etc.), but most of them are settled one way or another.

Yet very good reasons exist why people routinely prefer the litigation system rather than alternative dispute resolution systems. There are satisfactions to be gained—or thought to be available through the courts—that cannot be achieved (or that are thought not to be achievable) through alternative dispute resolution processes.

A court trial fulfills, or is thought to be capable of fulfilling, five needs that are usually absent in a mediated settlement: a sense of vindication, a sense of empowerment, a desire to be heard publicly, a desire for the particular dispute to receive the stamp of legitimacy, and the desire not only that justice be done but that it is manifestly seen to be done. Aggrieved litigants seek vindication, and further, they seek public vindication. That is to say, they want their "day in court," no matter what it costs. Perhaps they will not really achieve vindication, but there is always the chance that they might, and they see a trial as the best chance they have of achieving it. People do not necessarily approach their conflicts in purely rational terms; they have strong emotional interests to satisfy and a deep human desire to be proven right. They want to win, and they want someone else to lose. They want forever after to be able to tell themselves, their family, and their friends that they won their case. They want bragging rights. People will pay a high price for this, and will bear not only the cost of the litigation but also the risk of losing in order to attempt it.

People want to feel empowered; they want to feel that they can create an impact. When they walk into court for trial beside their hired champion, the attorney, and sit in the world of the courtroom looking up at the judge, they feel that the full authority of the state, which embodies the society in which they live, has interested itself in their particular conflict. And in fact it has, even though the particular judge may not quite see it that way.

Closely allied with these impulses is the desire to be heard, and to be heard in a public place. Today's courtroom represents the public square, the place where citizens gather to be heard and to vent their grievances. Fed on television drama, a person feels entitled to a day in court, and indeed is entitled to it. Even if the actual experience of testifying in a courtroom may not impart, to put it mildly, the sense of satisfaction that was anticipated in the beginning, at least that judge represents the authority of the state, with all its authority and legitimacy.

Justice is usually represented by the figure of a seated woman, blind-folded, holding a sword in one hand and the scales of justice in the other, but (as mentioned earlier) justice has an ugly little sister whose name is Revenge. One definition of justice is "the administering of deserved pun-ishment or reward." One definition of revenge is "to exact punishment or expiation of a wrong." If justice is the outward act, revenge is the inward feeling of satisfaction that accompanies it. Like Shylock, people "crave the law"; like Shylock, this is often a code word for revenge.

In summary, litigation offers satisfactions that other forms of conflict resolution usually cannot match: (1) vindication, (2) empowerment, (3) public hearing, (4) legitimacy, and (5) justice.

Mediation does not offer, or is thought not to offer, these satisfactions. Successful mediators need to understand and realize that the needs driving litigation are strongly felt and seek to find some way to accommodate them. It is because the existing trial court system is so broken in many ways that disputants seek alternative means to satisfy their needs.

Yet mediation offers satisfactions that the litigation system cannot hope to offer. These are (1) speed, (2) choice of mediator, (3) flexibility as to time and place, (4) low cost, (5) privacy and confidentiality, (6) mutually acceptable results, and (7) control of outcome.

The reality may not turn out the way the process was imagined, but that imagining remains a powerful lure. Many litigants are first-time entrants who have never done it before; most of their education may have been in the illusory processes of movie or television courtroom drama. If they go through with a trial, they often find that the real thing is slow, technical, cumbersome, tedious, and in the end emotionally disappointing.

That is why it is so easy to find great men writing cautions about litigation. Abraham Lincoln, U.S. President and a noted trial lawyer himself (he is estimated to have handled 5,000 cases) wrote, "Discourage litigation. Persuade your neighbors to compromise whenever you can. Point out to them how the nominal winner is often a real loser—in fees, expenses and waste of time."

Indeed, the theme of the disappointments of litigation is found as early as Cicero, the greatest lawyer of ancient Rome: "The litigious spirit is more often found with ignorance than with knowledge of the law."

Yet there are good reasons why the existing system has lasted so very long. Our society is said to be "litigious." That may be so, but it is the public that drives the litigation, with its demands for the kinds of satisfactions that the litigation process offers to provide, even with all its expenses, risks, and frequent disappointment. With skill, a mediator may seek to satisfy at least some of the satisfactions of litigation in addition to providing all the advantages of mediation.

Martin Luther King Jr. had his own reasons for insisting on law: "It may be true that the law cannot make a man love me, but it can keep him from lynching me, and I think that's pretty important."

The law is an elaborate creation. We may criticize it but we rely upon it for the preservation of civil society.

SIX

THE NATURE OF CONFLICT

The essence of *conflict* is collision. The root of the word is *fligere* (strike) + *con* (together). Although we tend to use the word *dispute* synonymously, its root is more benign: *putare* (consider or estimate) + *dis* (two ways, differently). At a physical level, the nature of conflict is expressed in the rule that two objects cannot occupy the same space at the same time; if they try to violate the rule, they collide. One might say the forces released in the Big Bang are fleeing the consequences of colliding in microspace, hence the expanding universe. This is conflict avoidance on a cosmic scale.

Living things are apt to collide in the competition for space and resources, but humans are more complicated. We have long memories, complex emotions, and nurture grudges, so we can fight about things that happened a long time ago; we can also fight about abstract ideas and beliefs.

The elements of conflict are past time, future time, wounds, desires, mind, and matter. Wounds exist in the past; desires exist in the future. A conflict may be played out on the twin planes of mind and matter.

TIME AS AN ELEMENT OF CONFLICT

Conflicts always contain time. Continued conflict is a way to drag the past into the future. The idea of justice is in essence a belief that past events can be "put right." We may also speak of the present moment, but the present moment is always in the process of becoming the past. Conflicts exist in the present, but they are always about something that is desired to happen or about something that already happened. That is why we try to know the future and the past.

The present moment is our point of perception; to the extent that the past exists at all, it can exist only in present perception, and to the extent that the future exists at all, it can exist only in present perception. But when one contemplates the nature of the present moment, it vanishes. It is always becoming the past and always rolling into the future. The only thing one can do with the present moment is experience it.

When people fight about the past, they are generally fighting about their wounds; when they fight about the future, they are generally fighting about their desires. Some conflicts pertain both to past and future; when wounds are mixed with desires, the entanglement is complex. Fights about the past are always about how to patch up the past so that wounded spirits may be satisfied, and fights over the future are always about who gets what, how much, and at what price. The most complex conflicts contain past time, future time, unhealed wounds, unfulfilled desires, conflicting doctrines and beliefs, and contest for territory and resources.

We approach the past by means of memory, physical and written records. Although we have only our stories about the past, they may be more or less accurate, depending on many factors, of which the most important is usually the passage of time. As memories fade, we have to rely on the written and physical record, and if there is no written record, we have only the physical record. Lawsuits involve an attempt to reconstruct the past; evidence is the law's method of reconstructing a past story.

The future is like the past in some ways. We have stories about the past and predictions about the future. We cannot remember the future, but we can predict it, and the accuracy of our predictions depends mainly upon time. Most people can predict what they are likely to be doing next week but not what they will be doing ten years ahead. No one can predict one hundred years ahead. When rapid change occurs, prediction becomes more difficult.

WOUNDS AND DESIRES

A "wound" may be psychological or material. The legal system compensates for material losses (economic damages) and for pain and suffering (noneconomic damages). Some wounds may have no material component.

"Desire" pertains to the future. Those who have no desires are either enlightened or apathetic. A desire may be for psychological or material satisfaction. It may be positive (to achieve gain) or negative (to cause loss).

MIND AND MATTER

These are separated conventionally, though material things may have an emotional or psychological component, and vice versa. The achievement of satisfaction often requires both to be addressed. A system that does not attempt to address both needs is incomplete, and means of doing so are then sought for "alternatively."

BELIEFS AND RESOURCES

Humans fight about ideas and beliefs. The inquisition of Galileo was about the earth's relationship to the sun. Bloody religious wars have been fought over quite abstruse points of doctrine. Today a battle is waged between Creationism and Darwinism. These are essentially conflicts in the realm of ideas. The desire for revenge is for mental satisfaction, though someone has written that it is like drinking poison and expecting the other fellow to die. People have always fought for the control of territory and natural resources. These are "who gets what" fights.

UNCERTAINTY

Whether we fight over the past or the future, we are dealing with uncertainty. Conflict increases the uncertainty of outcomes. Making peace is a way to diminish uncertainty. Negotiation involves an attempt to predict and influence the course of future events without conflict. Conflict management involves the development of systems to prevent conflict and to deal with it when it happens.

A person may also be in conflict with himself; these conflicts also are always about past wounds, future desires, or conflicting beliefs. The goal of conflict resolution is to heal past wounds, harmonize future desires, and reconcile conflicting beliefs.

There are two possible broad categories of subjects for conflict—things of the mind and physical resources. There is nothing else to fight about.

SUMMARY

On the physical level, we fight in time and space for control of matter and energy. We also fight for ideas and beliefs. We fight to heal wounds and fulfill desires. Conflicts may pertain to both past and future; the past contains wounds, the future contains desires. The most complex conflicts contain all variables at once: resources and ideas, past and future, wounds and desires, material and incorporeal. These involve a high degree of entanglement and congealed emotional energy. Dispute resolution is about untangling the contestants and releasing the energy.

SEVEN

IN DEFENSE OF CONFLICT

Some people have a hard time letting go of conflict. It is commonplace among psychotherapists that some patients cling to their problems. It seems that something is always better than nothing.

Most lawsuits yield readily to compromise because they are about risk assessment. Lawsuits for the most part are bargaining engines conducted with an eye to compromise. Although accurate risk assessment may be hard to achieve, it is nearly always attempted, and the tiny percentage of cases that go to trial are often a consequence of mistaken calculation by the losing party. In such clashes of interests, people pay attention to the money, but in a clash of fundamentals, people act as if they don't even believe in death, are immune to risk assessment, and will accept incalculable risk. These are the conflicts that we struggle to let go, but perhaps this is not a pathological condition but rather existential; perhaps these conflicts are "necessary."

Many writers equate enlightenment with lasting peace but utopian writers have always had a difficult time making heavenly peace sound interesting, and some have clearly preferred hell with its perpetual conflicts and faulty air-conditioning.

Perhaps it is not that we need less conflict but that we need more energy. It is not conflict that we wish to end, but only particular conflicts that we don't want anymore. We need a more effective mechanism to choose our conflicts and avoid those we do not want. We want to be rescued, sometimes. Conflicts are fine as long as we are winning. We generally approve of competition, yet competition is simply stylized and regulated conflict. Our society is organized around this principle. Who goes to a football game to watch them negotiate?

We love conflicts that require the hero to pass through the valley of death before triumphing. Boxing is pure expression of conflict. In A.J. Liebling's classic "The Sweet Science," we learn how the champion, Rocky Marciano, knocked out Ezzard Charles one night in New York's Madison Square Garden, that legendary crucible of triumph and disaster.

"Charles comes in in a good mental condition... Rocky is coming in. It is very hard to think when you are getting your brains knocked out, so Charles withdraws to consider the situation. Meanwhile, Marciano is still coming. Charles hits him a good right to the jaw, and Rocky hits him with a left hook and a right. First thing Charles knows, he is grabbing, and then he is just trying to hang on. Why? He don't know why. 'It is not like football,' Whitey said, kindly, like one trying to convey truth to little children, 'Rocky never gives you the ball.'"

Parties avoid trial by settling, as an exercise in risk management, and because for the most part it is only about adjusting the money. But we engage in conflict for more fundamental reasons, and the possibility of getting your ass kicked may be the admission ticket to the game of life. Life presents conflicts while death presents lasting peace, and there is something to be said for experiencing life before death.

We all enjoy the vicarious conflicts we engage in as spectators, and the players love the conflict too—except when they break a leg. Then they want people to rush onto the field with stretchers. Kids tilt headlong at life. They get into scrapes. After a while they have a setback and have to be extracted for a nap. Do they want lasting peace? I don't think so. There will be plenty of time for that. What kids want is lasting excitement. Mediators serve in the same capacity as stretcher-bearers, carrying people off the field when the game has become too much for them. What we would like is to pick and choose our conflicts, the ones where we end up as winners. But sometimes we meet Rocky, and he never gives us the ball. Then we get knocked silly, and that is when we pray for a mediator.

It is not all about conflict, thank goodness. Consider this from Haiti about a store clerk pulled from the rubble eleven days after the 2010 earthquake: "Lt. Col. Christophe Renou, a rescuer with the French team, called the three-hour effort a miracle as he was briefly overcome with emotion. Other members of the team—assisted by American and Greek workers—were seen weeping with joy following the rescue." Most touching was their openly emotional reaction to the rescue of a complete stranger. What was he to them that they should weep for him? Some conflicts may be necessary, but this rescue effort was about something more vital—the sense that we are all in this together. It is not a stark choice between competition and cooperation. Conflicts are inevitable, but cooperation is fundamental. Competition makes life exciting: cooperation makes life possible.

"What's Hecuba to him, or he to Hecuba
That he should weep for her? (Hamlet – Shakespeare)

EIGHT

NECESSARY CONFLICTS

Why does conflict persist? This is like asking, "Where does love go?" It touches the human condition near the core, a place where we get gloomy answers from great thinkers. "Life is suffering" is the first noble truth of Buddha. He lived about the same time as Heraclites who said: "War is the father and ruler of all things." St. Matthew in the New Testament agrees, "Ye shall hear of wars and rumors of wars" (Matt, 24, 6). The Abrahamic religions teach the Fall of man, and the English writer Thomas Hobbes offers a gloomy conclusion: "And the life of man—solitary, short, nasty, brutal, and short." Our personal and historical experience tells us that conflict does indeed persist.

Mediation, however, shares the sunny eighteenth-century optimism of the United States' Declaration of Independence affirmation of "life, liberty, and the pursuit of happiness." Does mediation believe in the possibility of permanent freedom from strife, or must it acknowledge something inevitable about conflict, something inherent in us that we cannot do without?

Questioning our persistent tendency to engage in conflict with each other, two qualities stand out as integral—entanglement and identity. We live entangled lives, yet we strive for personal identity. Our entanglements threaten our sense of ourselves. Conflicts are about entanglements gone wrong, and disentanglement is not easy. Shakespeare's *Richard III* thinks he can do it: "From this torment will I free myself, or hew my way out with the bloody axe," but he fails and gets his throat cut. Shakespeare's Macbeth sees no escape: "I am in blood stepped in so far that, Should I wade no more, Returning were as tedious as go o'er." The movie *Kramer vs. Kramer* is about identity; Mrs. Kramer feels compelled to desert her child because "I've always been someone's daughter, someone's wife, someone's mother." She flees to California to find out who she really is and finds out she really is a mother, so returns to get re-entangled with the child, but then… (complications ensue).

We are born entangled in the umbilical cord, and our connections bind us to life; Death carries a scythe to cut the cords—"Rosy lips and cheeks within his bending sickle's compass come." (Shakespeare: Sonnet 116) Even our genes express themselves in a double helix, an elegant entanglement. The intricacies of love and conflict occupy most of the space of our artistic heritage. What is curious is to discover exactly the same point made in quantum mechanics. "Entanglement is not one, but rather *the* characteristic trait of quantum mechanics." Yet seeking explanation we find another Nobel laureate, Richard Feynman, saying, "I think it is safe to say that no one understands quantum mechanics. You see my physics students don't understand it… that is because I don't understand it. Nobody does."

Feynman does offer some interpretation, from which it might appear that the entanglements of the quantum realm are not so different from our human experience: "I believe that all things are made of little particles that move around in perpetual motion, attracting each other when they are a little distance apart, but repelling upon being squeezed into one another." That pretty much sums up how we all live—moving around each other in perpetual motion, attracted and repelled, wanting each other yet jealous of our personal space, mingling and separating, alternating between lust and disgust, intimacy and estrangement.

Without closeness, which is the product of attraction, there can be no conflict, which is the product of repulsion. Eskimos don't get in fights with Papuans, because they are too far apart to get attracted in the first place. Marriage is hard work because it oscillates between attraction and repulsion. Violent crimes mostly happen between people who know each other, and the most common violence occurs within the family, which is one great big entanglement. Yet, unentangled people tend to be lonely and unhappy. Psychopaths are not entangled; where they seek closeness they achieve only violation—anyone "loved" by a psychopath is supremely threatened. The most unentangled humans are dead. The not-yet-born wait to embrace the entanglements of living. Physical attraction is the most entangling, for "how the devil could we exist, if our parents had never kissed?"

The poet T.S. Eliot sees the closest connection between love and conflict: "Love is the unfamiliar Name/Behind the hands that wove/The intolerable shirt of flame/Which human power cannot remove." The great scholar George Steiner agrees: "In essence, the constants of conflict and positive intimacy are the same."

The issue also exercised the dramatists of classical Greece, which was a civilization in perpetual conflict. They regarded certain conflicts as necessary and inescapable. Such conflicts are seen as "non-negotiable (whatever the many shades of accommodation between them) because together they constitute the means to self-knowledge. To arrive at oneself—the primordial journey—is to come up, polemically, against 'the other.'"

For anyone who would seek to mediate it, here is a synopsis of the play "Antigone" by Sophocles, in a certain family conflict. Polyneices, son of Oedipus, attacks the city of Thebes. His brother Eteocles, defending the city, meets Polyneices in battle and both die. Thebes is saved, and Creon, successor to Oedipus as king of Thebes, decrees the traitor be denied burial rites. Antigone, daughter of Oedipus and sister of the slain brothers, defies the decree. She buries her brother Polyneices to save his soul from endless torment. Creon sentences her to death for disobeying the law.

Why can't these two members of the royal family just get along? Why don't they work out a deal? Surely a mediator could help them—give a little, take a little, no need to hug, just sign on the dotted line. But they don't work out a deal. Antigone is confined in a living tomb and commits suicide, as does Creon's wife and his son, Haemon, who was Antigone's lover. Creon is as good as dead. The royals are hopelessly entangled and passionately, persuasively, and fatally stubborn. All five orders of conflict are implicated, which for Sophocles are as follows: between men and women, age and youth, the individual and the group, the living and the dead, and between mortals and god(s).

First, Antigone is a woman; her defiance of Creon's decree is intolerable. "So long as I am alive, no woman shall rule over me." Steiner writes of the relationship between a man and a woman: "They stand against each other as they stand close to each other… when they incur the perils of dialogue, men and women stand naked before each other… the immediacies and incommunicados of the words which they speak, whisper, hurl at each other, take us to the heart of our divided and polemic condition." Homer's much earlier epic opens with Helen's elopement and closes Clytemnestra's murder of Agamemnon. One could view all of civilization as an attempt to control the anarchic energies between men and women. The forces of society are harnessed to control the fusion but fail; the fallout is wrenching but creates the future. Then society musters itself once more, this time to respond to the question "Where did love go?" because the fission of separation is equally devastating, as we see in divorce statistics. Zeus may rule the heavens, but even he trembles before Aphrodite because her energies are unstoppable.

Secondly, Antigone is young and Creon is offended by her presumptuous challenge to one so much older; youth owes deference. In war, the old remain at home, the young are sent to die. Some have written that a person does not truly grow up until faced with the death of parents. One generation inflicts abuses on another. The old are pushed out to make way for the young. An entire society shortchanges the education of its young. The younger members of a family seek advantage of elderly relatives. Age is central in age discrimination and elder abuse situations. Shakespeare's King Lear is forced to acknowledge his impotence: "I am a very foolish, fond old man."

Thirdly, Antigone pits her personal conscience against Creon's conception of the state. Opposing her insistence on honoring the dictates of her inner voice, Creon is unyielding in his view that he, the King, knows what is best for Thebes, a place where heroes and traitors do not get the same treatment.

Fourthly, Antigone represents the claims of the dead, which may conflict with the interests of the living. Whatever their role in life, the dead share the kingdom of death, where different laws apply and must be honored. Antigone appeals to "the unwritten and unfailing laws of heaven." She is resolved that Polyneices must receive the proper rites, no matter what, and "no matter what" here means her death. Creon has no such delicacy of feeling for the departed. As far as he is concerned, his decrees are the law and apply to both the living and the dead.

Finally, the fifth order of confrontation is between men and god(s), and for Steiner, "the duel between men and gods is the most aggressively amorous known to experience." Creon seeks a commercial relationship with Zeus; he offers blasphemous reverence in expectation of reward. Antigone demands nothing and flinches from death even as she chooses it, but she places her action within the context of eternity, against which the temporalities of Creon can only splutter. We are not so comfortable talking of conflict between men and gods in a society either secular or monotheistic, but we do recognize the tension between time and eternity, immanence and transcendence, the mundane imperatives of our daily lives contrasted with what we all come to in the end. As the poet and preacher John Donne teaches: Death "comes equally to us all, and makes us all equal when it comes."

The movie *Babel* is about miscommunication leading to unintended and dire consequences. Even if we think we speak the same language, we frequently use the same words quite differently, and our disputes and antagonisms are based upon misinterpretations of what the other person said. The faculty of attentive listening is not so common. Most people most of the time have their attention solidly focused on themselves and not much attention is left over to listen closely to what the other person is saying. The possibilities for misunderstanding multiply. It becomes preferable not to speak at all. We fall silent.

Mediation does not usually directly involve such "necessary conflicts" but rather the clash of interests and the haggling of the marketplace, and is further constrained by the formalities of the setting. Just as abstract notions of justice rarely concern the lawyer in everyday practice, so the clash of ontological fundamentals may be only opaquely visible to the mediator.

Yet to the extent that mediation is a glass jar in which we are privileged to observe even somewhat formal attempts to find accommodation between conflicting actors, we can often notice, in their dogged refusal to take appropriate decisions in their own best interests, echoes of the five orders of confrontation set forth by Sophocles in the fifth century bce. To paraphrase quantum physicist Erwin Schrödinger we might conclude, "Entanglement is not one, but rather *the* characteristic trait of human interaction."

NINE

SEVEN QUALITIES OF THE COMPLETE MEDIATOR

A mediator needs to develop attentiveness, ethical consciousness, emotional intelligence, subject matter expertise, decisiveness, persistence, and courage.

ATTENTIVENESS

The most important ability for a mediator is to pay attention. One historian has written that our entire society suffers from attention deficit disorder. We live in information overload, thinking about what to do or say next.

The word *attend* is from the Latin *attendere* "to bend toward, to notice." Most people can pay attention for a few seconds; the required skill is to pay attention over time, to remain focused without having one's attention wander. If a mediator did nothing else but pay attention, the results would be remarkable.

Attention can be fixed or floating. It can be focused or diffused. It can be concentrated or peripheral. It can attend to one thing or several things. It can take in a single thing or many things at once. A person who practices paying attention will soon increase in ability and will experience increased awareness of what is going on. Paying attention is not terribly hard work; it has a light and airy quality. For example, a person absorbed in a book or a movie or a piece of music or a football game is paying close attention but without a great deal of effort. It is easy to pay attention when one is interested in the subject matter. It is possible for attention to be focused on something to the exclusion of everything else. It is possible for attention to roam like the beam of a flashlight. It is also possible to train one's attention to focus while remaining attentive to the periphery. The emotion accompanying attention is interest. Heightened interest may be experienced as enthusiasm or even excitement.

The opposite of attention is distraction. Different emotions may accompany distraction, including fear, but boredom is perhaps the most common.

Chaos is complex; order is simple. Parties in conflict are entangled in complexity. The job of the mediator is simplicity and disentanglement. To pay attention and let things unfold sounds deceptively easy but is a skill that takes practice to develop. Sometimes the mediator's ego gets in the way by wanting not only to achieve resolution but also to get credit for it; this is a distraction that detracts from paying attention. So is trying to think of what to do next, instead of just being attentive.

"Don't just do something; stand there."

—Numerous attributions

ETHICAL CONSCIOUSNESS

"A long habit of not thinking a thing wrong gives it a superficial appearance of being right."

—Thomas Paine, *Common Sense* (1776)

The subject of ethics concerns itself with action, with right or wrong conduct. Every day contains choices and decisions that implicate one's self and other people. All choices and decisions have consequences, and this is the subject of ethics. While everyone is aware of choice, not everyone is aware of the connection between choice and ethics. That may be because the subject of ethics is often relegated to actions that are immoral, illegal, dangerous, or fattening, thus restricting the subject of ethics to the consideration of wrongdoing. The better view of ethics is not only between clearly wrong and clearly virtuous but as the study of choices and consequences within a continuum from absolutely wrong to absolutely right.

Concern with ethics was never better expressed than by John Bunyan in the opening paragraph of his great work "Pilgrim's Progress," begun in Bedford jail and published in 1678.

> *"And behold, I saw a man clothed with rags standing in a certain place, with his face from his own house, a book in his hand, and a great burden upon his back. I watched, and beheld him open the book and read therein, and as he read he wept and trembled, and not being longer able to contain, he brake out with a lamentable cry, saying: 'What shall I do?'"*
>
> *—Pilgrim's Progress*

The question is not "Who am I?" or "Where have I come from?" or "Why do I have to die?" or "What is my destiny?" but "What shall I do?" That question contains two qualities: it refers to action and to the future. Ethics concerns itself with right action or better action. It pertains to the mediator who has a duty to be impartial as between the parties. Mediators are also called "neutrals," and although that word has stuck, it does not successfully describe the function of a mediator.

Neutral is a condition in which the third party stays out of the conflict, giving no help to either side. If a mediator were truly neutral, there would be little point in seeking her assistance; the parties could use a stuffed doll instead.

> *"The hottest place in Hell is reserved for those who remain neutral in times of great moral conflict."*
>
> *—attributed to Dante Alighieri and others*

Impartial is a different word with a different meaning. It means "not partial or biased; fair, just." Although a judge has the responsibility of judgment, she is required to be impartial at the start of a case, yet is entirely partial by the end. The act of judgment is to choose one side. That is the function of a judge, but not a mediator. As used in connection with mediation, "impartiality" suggests full yet even-handed involvement, giving as much assistance as ethically possible to all sides in the conflict. Of course, the question always is, How much is ethically possible? That is why the distinction between evaluative and facilitative mediation is not merely a matter of style. A facilitative mediator has made the choice not to evaluate for the parties, whereas an evaluative mediator is willing to state an opinion. Such decisions necessarily involve considerations of right or wrong conduct in the context of mediation.

There is always a power imbalance between parties to a dispute. Does the mediator seek to address, and adjust, the power imbalance by lending a bit more weight to the weaker side? Is such "tipping the scales" in favor of greater balance between the parties to be considered an exercise in partiality or impartiality? Sometimes one party appears with an attorney, the other without one; the person with the attorney is nearly always at an advantage. Should the mediator attempt to redress the power imbalance by helping the unrepresented party understand the legal ramifications of the situation, and the possible perils buried within it? Or is the correct action simply to recognize the power imbalance and do nothing to prejudice the stronger position of one of the parties?

What if both parties are represented, one by an attorney who knows the file and the other by an attorney who is clearly unprepared? Should an experienced mediator lend a hand to an inexperienced lawyer or unrepresented party? What if one attorney has overlooked something that will tilt the balance of the negotiation in favor of her client? What is the mediator's responsibility?

Is impartiality even possible, particularly after meeting the disputants and hearing their respective stories? Does the mediator not naturally incline to one side or the other, if only because one side has a better case? The Model Standards of Mediation Practice simply advise, "A mediator shall avoid conduct that gives the appearance of partiality to towards one of the parties." How does one reconcile that standard with the duty of honesty and transparency? This is not the problem of bias or prejudice, which is conceptually simple because it is clearly not acceptable, but a question of ethical conduct. Because after the two sides of a conflict are laid out, often it is plain that one side has the better of it; then should the mediator close her eyes to the obvious and join the parties in denial or simply dissemble by presenting a mask of an impartiality she does not feel? And if not, then what is she to do? This is the concern of ethics.

"Every word is a bias or inclination."

—attributed to Nietzsche

During the course of the mediation, a mediator may come to have a clear view of the respective merits of the parties' positions. Should she express her own views to the parties? Sometimes parties want such an evaluation from the mediator, but what if the parties do not ask for an evaluation? What if one party is stubborn in insisting on a position that is wrong, unjust, and cannot possibly win? Should the mediator take that person to one side, privately, and explain to him the realities of the situation?

Mediation rests on three essentials: impartiality, confidentiality, and voluntary participation. What if one party desires to speak privately with the mediator and then confesses to a crime? What if the confession involves an offence with a child? What is the mediator's obligation? These are all ethical issues.

EMOTIONAL INTELLIGENCE

"Le coeur a ses raisons que le raison ne connait pas."

—Pascal, 1632

"The heart has its reasons that reason does not comprehend." Blaise Pascal's aphorism is the subject of emotional intelligence. The phrase "emotional intelligence" refers to an ability that is becoming more valued though not much taught in our society and educational systems. The phrase itself is something of a deliberate oxymoron, because the emotions are normally distinguished from the activity of the intelligence; it expresses the need to relate empathetically to what is being communicated by another person, including the emotional drives underlying such communication.

The topic of "body language" concerns itself with developing emotional intelligence, which is not an abstract or esoteric ability but can easily be learned by taking the trouble closely to observe the behavior of other people. It helps the mediator to learn to relate empathetically to the participants if they are to feel they have truly been heard in expressing their grievances and needs, which is an essential step in the mediation process because it leads to willingness to negotiate a resolution.

Any person is either more or less open, or more or less concealed. Some people deliberately conceal themselves in an effort to deceive, whereas others just do not know how to be more open. The latter are not concealing so much as protecting themselves. Some people pretend to be open while in fact concealing a great deal. Some people deliberately notice much while revealing little; this is a stratagem. Everyone is on a continuum between completely closed and completely open, and people may vary a great deal in the course of an hour as to how much they are willing to reveal, and how much they wish to conceal.

The mediator is not a therapist and is not so much trying to achieve a breakthrough in openness for its own sake as to bring about sufficient communication to make resolution possible. The kind of resolution being sought in a given dispute determines the level of openness required. Evaluative mediation requires the least communication, transformative mediation the most. Thus, mediators and participants who seek transformative change may expect to take a good deal longer than a regular mediation. Where parties have come together to talk about their differences and negotiate settlement or resolution, the mediator is interested only in achieving enough communication between them that they can achieve the result they came for.

SUBJECT MATTER EXPERTISE

Subject matter expertise can be learned by a mediator and means expertise in the subject matter of the particular dispute, for example, construction, divorce and family relationships, childcare, business and commercial, contracts, labor relations, environmental, government, torts, real estate, neighborhood, or international relations.

Parties to a dispute, in choosing a mediator, often deliberately seek some subject matter experience, and it is helpful for a mediator to acquire and therefore be able to mediate disputes in that subject area.

However, it will be found, once the mediator has become proficient in the craft of mediation, that those skills can be applied across a wide variety of subject matters. If a mediator gets results, that is due to her mediation expertise rather than subject matter expertise. With no subject matter expertise at all, the mediator may experience difficulty communicating with the parties in a credible manner. With great subject matter expertise but no mediation skills, the mediator may be able to communicate with the parties but lack the ability to focus them on resolution. The expertise of the mediator is in dispute resolution, which is applicable across many subject matters; there is no limit to that level of expertise. Even if the mediator is an expert in a given subject matter, she will not attain the same level of knowledge of a particular dispute as the parties who have been living with it. The mediator must know enough of the facts, and enough of the subject matter, to ensure that her mediation expertise will be effectively brought to bear.

DECISIVENESS

Decisiveness is essential in a mediator because she cannot allow a mediation to wallow without the parties becoming impatient, except in those relatively uncommon instances in which the mediation is designed to be "transformational" and partakes of many of the qualities of therapy. The mediator has to decide whom to speak to, when to speak to them, what to say to them, and how much to allow them to say because she has an obligation to create a momentum and keep it going. There is a purpose in view, and there is usually a time limit. Unless the parties feel they are making some progress, they are likely to become discouraged and the mediation may fail to achieve its purpose, which is to effect resolution.

PERSISTENCE

As Winston Churchill said, "Never give up. Never, never, never, never, never." Yet someone else said: "You've got to know when to fold them," meaning to walk away. Whole books are written about persistence. Everyone agrees that persistence is critical in any endeavor. That is because most of us are not very persistent; we are inclined to give up. Because a conflict has its own momentum, its own internal dynamics, its own perceived dividend, and its own persistence, it takes a lot of energy to create countermomentum and the energy to bring it to an end. For participants, it may take less energy just to keep slogging away. The participants may wish an end to the conflict, yet still they cannot generate enough willpower to achieve closure. The presence of a mediator tips the scales, provided she is persistent. The great American comedian W.C. Fields had a different view: "If at first you don't succeed, try and try again. Then quit. No use being a damn fool about it."

COURAGE

A mediator needs to have some guts, as she may have to tell the truth to someone or everyone and telling the truth can be quite challenging. It is also not easy to write anything about courage that is neither sentimental nor trite, but others have tried. Here is a small selection.

"Courage is going from failure to failure without losing enthusiasm."
—Winston Churchill, British statesman

"Courage is the price that Life exacts for granting peace."
—Amelia Earhart, American aviation pioneer

"To see what is right and not to do it is want of courage."
—Confucius, Chinese philosopher

"Life shrinks or expands in proportion to one's courage."
—Anaïs Nin, French writer

"Courage is the art of being the only one who knows you're scared to death."

—Earl Wilson, American journalist

In summary, these seven qualities are skills that can be learned and developed. Attentiveness is the foundation of communication skills but must be combined with decisiveness because it is up to the mediator to make things happen. Action must happen, but it must be right action, which is the subject of ethics. The mediator must develop sensitivities that are not accessible to pure reason, and this is the subject of emotional intelligence. The mediator must be able to talk the same language as the disputants, which means some subject matter expertise. The mediator must act decisively to move the disputants toward a result not entirely satisfactory to any of them and must persist when they have given up hope of resolution. A mediator is not exactly a lion tamer, but it helps to have a little courage, because sometimes one has to risk being authentic and then anything can happen.

The scarcity of these qualities is why the mediation is happening at all. The mediator supplies what is missing to enable the disputants to settle their dispute and move on with their lives.

It has been said that people get attached to their conflicts and find it hard to give them up, even if they want to. It is a service to people to disentangle them; we call this resolution, or peace. General Sherman marched through Georgia, laying waste the countryside but with minimal loss of human life on either side, and thus helped end the American Civil War. Mediators are needed to help end conflicts and must do so without ravaging the countryside.

"War is hell."

—General William Tecumseh Sherman

TEN

LISTENING, ACKNOWLEDGING, QUESTIONING

LISTENING

A mediator must listen. Listening is among the most important skills of a mediator. Active listening shows respect. A great deal can be accomplished by listening. It is also of critical importance to let the person who is speaking know that you are listening to him or her; this is acknowledgment.

Acknowledgment does not mean agreement. Acknowledgment merely means that you are carefully listening to what the person has to say. When people say they "want their day in court," they often mean that they want to be listened to. It is a sad fact that although lawyers are trained to ask questions in order to elicit the essential facts of a dispute, often the attorney has neither the time nor the inclination really to listen to the client's concerns. The reason for this is that clients often want to communicate a great many matters that are not relevant, and attorneys are not willing to act as therapists. Neither is the mediator a therapist. A person may go to a therapist in order to explore an inner concerns and anguish, and the therapeutic relationship may be an ongoing relationship with a goal to achieve in the patient relief of mental suffering and feelings of well-being or self-esteem. The work of psychotherapists, clinical psychologists, and psychiatrists, according to one playwright is to:

> *"Minister to a mind diseased, Pluck from the memory a rooted sorrow, Raze out the written troubles of the brain, And with some sweet oblivious antidote, Cleanse the stuffed bosom of that perilous stuff which weighs upon the heart."*

—Macbeth (Shakespeare)

The mediator has a less daunting, more immediate task. The mediator's responsibility is to achieve in a limited time frame a result, settlement, a resolution, and in some instances a reconciliation. Although parties may experience great relief and satisfaction resulting from a mediated resolution or reconciliation, it is a different discipline than therapy. The therapist concentrates entirely on her patient; the mediator is an impartial intermediary. For both the therapist and the mediator, active listening is a vital skill.

A litigant who expects to be listened to closely, heard, and acknowledged during his or her day in court will be sadly disappointed with the system. Litigants in the witness box are expected, and indeed required, to answer the question put to them—and only that question. If they deviate, they are likely to be admonished by the judge. They are subject to hostile cross-examination. The court is aiming for a legal result, and judges do not act as therapists.

Therefore, the mediator must learn, first and foremost, to listen. Next, the mediator must learn to walk a fine line between attempting to function as a therapist and acting too abruptly. Further, the mediator must learn to acknowledge the person speaking without being annoying about it. For example, some listeners continuously nod their heads when they are being spoken to; this can be quite irritating to the speaker. Some pseudo-listeners try to fake it; they put on a serious expression, and may even look the speaker in the eye, but their mind and their attention is elsewhere. Some people listen with one ear while in reality they are trying to work out what to say next or what to do next. Pure listening is simply that, and nothing more.

Curiously enough, if you give a person your entire attention, they are more likely to say what they have to say in a shorter time than if you allow your attention to wander. Intense, active listening is so rare in our society that it is quite a surprise to a distraught litigant to be listened to with the full attention of the mediator on him or her.

How does the mediator respond to an outburst of grief or, quite frequently, grief mixed with a level of anger? The answer is that it is not necessary to comfort or console a person; it may be counterproductive and may have ethical implications as a breach of impartiality. It is not necessary to do anything other than listen to him or her with the utmost respect. Listening to a person is in itself a form of showing respect. It is respectful to listen carefully, and if the communication is accompanied by a display of emotion, it remains the correct thing to do merely to listen, acknowledge, and show respect. A display of emotion is after all nothing more or less than a form of communication. In our society, people are easily disturbed by displays of emotion; it upsets the social norm. But there is no need for it to upset the mediator.

The way to learn how to listen is to listen, and to continue practicing listening. It is at the same time very simple and very difficult. It can also be intense and exhausting. In mediation that may last five or six hours, the mediator is likely to spend the majority of the time listening intently. If she does this, the participants are likely to feel that they have indeed had the equivalent of their day in court, and you have spared them the disappointment of finding out what a day in court is really like. They will feel that they have been understood, which is a great blessing. But don't make the mistake of expecting them to understand you in return; ego in a mediator is a losing proposition.

ACKNOWLEDGING

It is not enough to listen; it is necessary also to acknowledge. The person must feel that she has been understood. The way to accomplish this is by acknowledgment.

The simplest form of acknowledgment is to say something like "Okay" or "Thank you" or "I heard you" or "I appreciate you telling me that" or "I understand what you are telling me."

REFRAMING

It is also a commonly used technique to restate what the person has just said, that is to say, to repeat it back to him or her in your own words but in such a way as to make it clear that you have understood what has been said to you. This is also called reframing, paraphrasing, and summarizing. It is an important skill, and it is also important not to overdo it. It can become annoying if the mediator reframes everything that has been said to him or her.

In most discussions, a simple acknowledgment is sufficient. However, when a person has been speaking for a certain length of time, it is helpful not only to the speaker but also to the mediator for the mediator to say something such as "I want to summarize that so that we can both be sure that I have fully heard and understood what you wanted to say." The way to learn restatement/reframing/paraphrasing/summarizing is simply to practice doing it.

Excessive nodding of the head is annoying. It usually means, or is interpreted as meaning, that a person is pretending to listen, or it may be just a nervous habit.

QUESTIONING

There are three types of questions that can be asked: open-ended questions, closed questions, and leading questions.

A *closed question* seeks a specific answer and may often seek a *yes* or *no* answer. Examples are "How old are you?" "Am I acceptable as a mediator in this situation?" "When did you first become aware of this problem?" As can be seen, these are questions that mostly rely upon the four W's: who, what, where, and when. If you asked a question beginning with "why," you are likely to receive a more expansive answer.

An *open question* provides the opportunity for a response in the nature of a narrative, certainly a more expansive response than if sought when the question is closed, and it may result in the responder giving you more information. For example, "How have you enjoyed working here?" "Please describe what you were doing at the time?" "What would you describe are the benefits of having worked in this job for so long?"

A *leading question* is the type of questioning generally employed by cross-examiners, and leading questions may be perceived as being hostile, or at least unfriendly, because they appear to, and are often intended to, box in the responder. "You enjoyed it, didn't you?" "You arrived at 9:00 a.m. on the morning in question, isn't that correct?"

The mediator will usually ask open questions to start the mediation. This serves two purposes: it gives the mediator an opportunity to learn more about the matter at hand, and it invites communication. When people are invited to communicate, generally they respond and, if they are listened to, they will enjoy responding. It is a universal human trait to wish to be heard.

As the mediation continues, the mediator may ask more closed questions, particularly questions that ask for clarification. "Which strategies do you consider to be appropriate for this task?" "What terms did you have in mind?" "What is your demand?" "What is your offer?"

POLITENESS

Politeness will take you a long way as a mediator and as a human being. Greeting each person with courtesy, looking them in the eyes (without staring) as you shake their hands, giving each person your full attention, thanking them for being there, offering them refreshment, showing them to their seats—these are valuable skills easy to learn and practice yet curiously in short supply in our fast-paced society. Smile. In the presence of courtesy and consideration, people start to relax, find safety and open up; apart from being the right way to behave, it makes the mediator's task a lot easier.

The power of the mediator is the power of communication. The task of the mediation is to get the disputants focused, then to get them communicating and keep them at it. To do this, the mediator must master communication skills.

"Begin each day with a smile. Get it over with early."

—W.C. Fields, American comedian

ELEVEN

BODY LANGUAGE AND CREATING TRUST

"There's no art to find the mind's construction in the face."

—Macbeth (Shakespeare)

A mediator can use her own body language to send nonverbal cues to participants, put them at their ease, and commence the process of creating trust. Here are five simple, unobtrusive, and effective techniques:

1. Breathe slowly and peacefully. Although it may seem strange at first, making a conscious effort to control your breathing will reduce stress and impact mediation participants in a positive way. When people are apprehensive and stressed, they tend to breathe shallowly. When they are very nervous, they may even start to breathe in short, quick gasps. Your physical posture or demeanor affects your mood. It will favorably impact others if you stand or sit up straight; smile; and straighten, rather than hunch, your shoulders. If you are feeling uneasy or insecure in the presence of the participants, attend first to your own physical posture, and you will notice not only a difference in yourself but also a more relaxed feeling in the participants. A successful mediator conveys an attitude of

confidence, friendly yet business-like, which is an important step in helping participants feel comfortable with the mediator.

2. Eye contact. There are four possible forms of eye behavior: (a) no contact; (b) shiftily looking here and there; (c) heavy staring; and (d) relaxed, open, and friendly eye contact. No eye contact at all is perceived in Western cultures as refusal to make contact. A shifty-eyed person is perceived as untrustworthy, but liars can sometimes overcompensate by staring fixedly at the other person. Staring fixedly into someone's eyes can be construed as aggression, and in the animal kingdom or in bars, it is often seen as a challenge.

    The mediator does well to take her cues from each party, as each person has a certain comfort level, and mirroring it will tend to establish rapport. Eye contact is a sign of recognition; in most cultures, it is respectful to seek eye contact, but there is no need to lock on to the other person like a ground-to-air missile. If you want someone to feel noticed, gently focus your right eye on that person's right eye for a few seconds, and then let your focus be directed at the upper half of the person's face, above the bridge of the nose, in a relaxed, nonconfrontational manner.

    Degree of eye contact is also a function of status. In hierarchical societies, the lowly do not seek eye contact with the mighty. To see an example of this, watch the movie *The Madness of King George*; it was an unforgivable breach of etiquette to make eye contact with the king, yet when George III was declared insane, his physician locked eyes with his patient, causing the king to protest in fury.

    In Los Angeles, a Japanese gardener became involved in a dispute with his employer. At the hearing, the gardener would not look at either his employer or the mediator and would not even approach the conference table, but remained seated by the wall. This was an expression of perceived hierarchical differences—a difficult problem for the arbitrator used to the ways of freewheeling American democracy.

3. Body position. Do not keep your arms crossed and, for the most part, do not cross your legs. Turn your body toward the parties to

demonstrate receptivity. A person with something to hide will tend to try to hide or shield her body, which inhibits the perception of openness. For the same reason, do not engage in habits like twisting hair, tapping your feet or your fingers, or nail biting, because those actions are perceived as signs of anxiety.

4. Smile. Nothing is worse than a fake smile, and nothing better than a genuine one. In spite of George Burns' famous joke about faking sincerity, it is better not to smile at all than to fake it, because it is always obvious. There is nothing wrong with a polite smile, a respectful smile, a slight smile, or any smile that is not insincere. When meeting people for the first time, a broad smile may well be perceived as inappropriate in the situation. For what may be complex social reasons, women tend to smile more readily than men; just look for a while at your television set, watching for the different behavior patterns of men and women.

5. Mirror and match. This is an important technique because it is so powerful. It can also backfire if it is overdone or too obvious. Watch what the other person is doing, literally, with her own body: Is she leaning forward or backward? Is her voice well modulated, or high-pitched or stressed, or interested, or frightened or angry? At what speed is she speaking? Is she leaning to the left or to the right? What is she doing with her legs, arms, torso, shoulders, and face? Some of her body language may be negative; do not copy negative body language, because it is likely to backfire. Instead, copy positive body language and tone of voice with your own posture and verbal responses. She will begin to feel the remarkable effect that you are "in sync" with her, and she will start to open up to you. This is effective in two ways: it make her feel good not only about herself but also about being in your presence.

Body postures are all variations of open or closed. Both anger and fear are manifested in closed posture, as are discouragement or despondency. Examples of closed posture are hunched shoulders; tensed muscles, including facial muscles; a drooped head; and the chest drawn inward. An open posture has straight shoulders, relaxed muscles, a straight head, a relaxed mouth, and a forward chest.

The four most obvious body postures are as follows:

1. Closed posture, leaning forward: a sign that the person is not paying attention and is perhaps disbelieving or emotional. This is a combative posture.

2. Closed posture, leaning back: a sign that the person would rather not be there at all. It is an indication of a desire to escape, and it is what the mediator least wants to see. It is more difficult to overcome than the first posture and needs to be attended to attentively and as soon as possible.

3. Open posture, leaning back: a sign that the person is considering the situation and reflecting upon it. The mediator takes this as a good sign and does not interrupt.

4. Open posture, leaning forward: a sign that the person is responsive to what is being said. Clearly the goal of the mediator is to achieve a change from closed posture to open posture. Sometimes, the mediator is called upon to deliver a "reality check" to one or both participants, and that will not go down well, or be accepted at all, unless the participants are receptive to the mediator and believe that she is impartially doing her best.

Open palms are regarded as a sign of receptivity. Unless someone is quite sophisticated in the practice of deceit, she will not display open palms in an attempt to deceive.

Signs of rejection are (1) touching or rubbing the nose, (2) crossing arms or legs, and (c) rubbing hands or tugging at the ear. However, women frequently cross their legs in social situations, and the mediator should not construe this as defensiveness or rejection. Men also cross their legs for reasons of habit or comfort. The mediator, once she practices noticing these various body cues, soon learns to distinguish between social habits and signs of acceptance or rejection.

No one gets it right all the time.

In 1967, in the *Journal of Personality and Social Psychology* and the *Journal of Consulting Psychology*, Albert Mehrabian of the University College of Los Angeles published the findings of two studies suggesting that people derive their understanding of a communication as follows: 7% from the words, 38% from the tone of voice, and 55% from body language. This is sometimes called the "rule of 55/38/7." If this were entirely true, people need hardly bother to use words at all, but an observer will soon discover that body language constitutes a significant part of a person's communication. This is especially true in a mediated negotiation, because negotiating parties often send mixed messages and often intend to deceive in the hope of improving their bargaining positions. Close attention to body language gives the mediator valuable information as to what is really going on.

GENDER DIFFERENCES

Here is a well-known experiment: Two chairs are placed randomly in an otherwise empty room. The experimenter (psychologist) watches behind a one-way mirror. Two four-year-old girls are let into the room. They immediately place the chairs facing each other and sit with their knees touching, looking each other in the face, and commence their communication together.

The next experiment is the same, except with two four-year-old boys. The boys place the chairs spaced widely apart, at a 45-degree angle facing outward; then, without really looking at each other, one says, "What game shall we play?" This experiment was conducted as part of the age-old quest to determine whether gender differences are the result of nature or nurture. As usual with the nature–nurture debate, the results, though striking in what was observed, are inconclusive as to causation.

However, the mediator, in observing body language, needs to take into account the observed difference between men and women. It is said that women communicate to establish rapport with each other, and part of the process of the manner in which women communicate is that they do not mind interrupting or being interrupted and, indeed, see that kind of dynamic interaction as helpful to the process of establishing rapport.

Men, on the other hand, are said to communicate in order to "report" with each other—in other words, to give an account of events. Generally, men do not care to be interrupted but would prefer to wait until they have completed one thought before the other party responds. The mediator, whether male or female, does well to bear in mind these differences in the manner in which the genders tend to conduct communication with each other.

Where lawyers are involved, whether male or female, their training as lawyers tends to supersede this dynamic so that one might expect attorneys to behave more like each other, no matter whether they are male or female, but the style of communication in law is biased toward the male gender because it has been only relatively recently that women were admitted to the practice of law.

In interpreting body language, it should be noted that women have been found to be more communicative in general than men and to use both verbal and nonverbal cues more frequently than men. One study found that, upon entering a room, men displayed an average of twelve body movements, whereas women exhibited twenty-seven distinctive body movements, which is quite a difference. In the conduct of negotiation, participants are intensely interested in the power and status of the negotiating parties, for the obvious reason that those with power have the greater advantage. This initially works to the disadvantage of women because it has been found that, when observers are asked to rate power and status, they rate those who display fewer physical gestures higher than those people who are more animated. The lesson might be that women who negotiate should consciously control their body movements, but the contrary view is that women do better if they "are themselves" rather than attempting to conform to stereotype.

It is best to play to one's strengths, not to other people's stereotypes. Consider Cleopatra, whose hold on the world's imagination has lasted two thousand years and who, at least in Shakespeare's play, does not disdain animated movement:

"I saw her once hop forty paces through the public street, and having lost her breath, she spoke and panted... age cannot wither her, nor custom stale her infinite variety." - Antony and Cleopatra (Shakespeare)

In his song from *My Fair Lady*, Professor Higgins asks why a woman isn't more like a man, but in the end he says that he has become accustomed to her face; he means that he loves her. A person always does better in his or her own skin than trying to occupy someone else's skin to satisfy some prejudice. Initial perceptions are mostly the result of stereotyping. The best negotiators find their own style. The best mediators do the same.

CULTURAL DIFFERENCES

There is a great variety in body language across different cultures, and a mediator does well to remember that gestures acceptable in one culture are taken as insulting in another. But most people in mediation are ready to conform to the cultural behaviors of the country in which the mediation is located. The way for a mediator to proceed when faced with cultural difference is to observe the behavior of each person carefully and mirror it, being mindful always to show respect.

For example, in some far-eastern countries, people often bow rather than shake hands and may feel more comfortable with a bow than with a handshake. People from different cultures have different cultural norms as to the space they prefer to keep from one another, some closer, some more distant. The mediator needs simply to mirror the preferences of participants.

In India, people often greet each other by placing their hands in a prayer position in the center of the chest, with the head slightly bowed. In Middle Eastern countries, greeting is often done by way of a *salaam*, in which the right hand touches first the heart, then the forehead. In Japan and Korea, when parties shake hands, they are cautious about eye contact, because eye contact may be seen as intimidating. In France, people may greet each other with a kiss on both cheeks. In Russia, a hug often accompanies a handshake, and in some countries, a handshake with a right hand is often accompanied by touching the right arm with the left hand in a gesture of intimacy.

All over the world, there are different methods of greeting. It is not necessary for a mediator to learn all of these, but the closer the mediator observes his guests, and the more willing he is to mirror their conduct, the sooner he will establish rapport with them.

Finger pointing or shaking one's finger at another is never a good idea.

Here is an example of an error recovered from, and the fruits of mirroring: The participant was from a Middle Eastern country. The mediator asked conversationally, "Where are you from?" The participant seemed to resent the question, and asked, "Why do you ask?" "Oh, I was just making conversation." "I am an American citizen. I have been here for 25 years." That was a rocky start, but over the course of some hours, the mediator was polite and respectful to the participant, winning his trust to such a degree that, toward the end, the participant asked the mediator for his evaluation, which the mediator gave. The participant was not happy with the evaluation but said, "I will do as you say, because you are my elder brother," in the circumstances an unusual and even extraordinary thing to hear. Although a facilitative mediator might regard such an evaluation as impermissible, it resulted in settlement that all participants found satisfactory after an arduous, costly dispute.

OTHER CLUES

More subtle clues include the following:

Dilated pupils. If a person looks you straight in the eye and lies, the pupils will dilate involuntarily.

Tiny facial expressions. When a person tells a lie, a micromovement of facial muscles will occur—an eyebrow movement, a small frown, a lip gesture—lasting less than half a second. There are ninety muscles in the face; thirty are used for expressing emotion, and many facial and other muscles are not under voluntary control.

Words not matching body language. When people negotiate, they are negotiating with the mediator as well as each other, and with their own inner impulses. The watchwords for the mediator are *listen* and *watch*. More frequent than outright lies are incomplete truths. Negotiators often hide their bargaining position from the mediator, and an observant mediator will pick up all sorts of clues from body language to aid her on the road to closure.

A person can always control the words that come out of her mouth, but body language is mostly involuntary and is very hard to control for an extended period. Some people possess no feelings of guilt, shame, or remorse and an extraordinary ability to lie with a straight face.

Why, I can smile, and murder whiles I smile,
And cry "Content" to that which grieves my heart,
And wet my cheeks with artificial tears,
And frame my face to all occasions.
Henry IV, Part 2

—Shakespeare

THE IMPORTANCE OF CONTEXT

Body language varies according to context:

- Young people behave differently around parents than friends.

- College students behave differently around professors than dorm buddies.

- Men behave differently with one another than if women are present, and vice versa.

In a professional setting, such as mediation, parties usually behave with more constraint than in a more relaxed setting.

SUMMARY

1. Women are often more expressive than men.

2. Habitual body language varies between cultures, and the same gesture can mean something quite different.

3. The setting always counts, such as the degree of formality of the occasion and perceived differences in social status, gender, ethnic, culture, and age differences.

4. Respectful politeness goes a long way and will ease the mediator past many difficult situations. Always greet everyone, and always stand to greet anyone. Mirror the person in front of you without affectation or caricature.

TWELVE
ATTITUDES, EMOTIONS, AND FEELINGS

Humans experience a range of emotions. *Anger* is also called rage, fury, annoyance, irritation, or frustration, depending on the intensity. *Fear* is also expressed as nervousness, apprehension, worry, or concern. *Grief* includes sadness, upset, feeling of loss, or mourning. *Apathy* is also called loss of affect, feeling of deadness. *Boredom* includes wandering attention, impatience. *Interest* is not always identified as an emotion; it may be strong, bordering on enthusiasm, or mild.

Emotions include enthusiasm (from the Greek *enthusiasmos* "possession by a god"), joy, ecstasy, excitement, interest, and boredom.

Emotions also include anger, fear, grief, pain, shame, blame, propitiation, resentment, and apathy.

Basic simplification: glad, sad, mad, and scared.

Boredom is on the borderline between anger and interest. Children are prone to boredom, as in "Mom, there's nothing to do," but a child may pass from boredom to active interest in the twinkling of an eye. Boredom sometimes seems like apathy, and vice versa, but they are by no means the same. In our society, people routinely try to disguise their emotions. If someone says, "I'm disappointed that the other side responded in such and such way," that is coded language meaning "I'm angry."

Many people react to an unwanted situation with either shame (wrongly targeting oneself) or blame (wrongly targeting someone else). In mediations, each side often begins by blaming the other.

Some people are simply "absent"; no one at home. Then it is not possible to spot any emotion. What is the emotional state of a sleeping person?

Love is not an emotion, though may be accompanied by various emotions. Neither is hate. It is an attitude. Hate may be fueled by anger, fear, grief, pain, envy, or any negative emotion. The desire for revenge is based on hate, as Iago says in Shakepeare's Othello: "I have told thee often, and I retell thee again and again, I hate the Moor.... Let us be conjunctive in our revenge against him." (Act 1, Scene 3)

Expressed as emotion, energy may be directed forward (anger, interest, enthusiasm) or backward (fear), or be motionlessness (grief, apathy).

In any mediation, all persons enter the room with a mixture of attitudes, emotions, and feelings. In our society, it is a culturally imposed habit to suppress or inhibit these attitudes, emotions, and feelings. But they are nonetheless present.

Attitude is better understood as a viewpoint, or perspective, or way of looking at the world. Attitude is usually qualified with an adjective, such as an amiable attitude, a defiant attitude, a hostile attitude, a competitive attitude, a cooperative attitude. Every person in every mediation, indeed every person in every situation, is presenting a certain face toward the world and that is his or her attitude, for example, a winning attitude, a negative attitude, a coquettish attitude, a conniving attitude, an arrogant attitude, a humble attitude, and so on. What we want in mediation is a businesslike attitude, moving from competitive to cooperative. Even so, the parties may remain competitive and still settle the dispute.

Parties to any dispute fall into two broad and fundamental categories.

The first category consists of people who were not in any kind of prior relationship get themselves entangled together in a dispute. Their relationship consists entirely of the dispute and, when the dispute is resolved, their relationship will be at an end. Into this category fall many litigated disputes, such as auto accidents.

The second category of dispute consists of people who have an ongoing relationship and either desire or are obliged to continue an ongoing relationship after the dispute is resolved. Into this second category fall divorces, where there are children involved; after the divorce, it is necessary for the parties to maintain a relationship with each other for the sake of the children. There are many instances of business disputes, where the parties will ideally want to maintain or recommence a relationship with each other once they have settled the particular dispute.

The method of handling these two disparate categories is entirely different. In the first case, the parties can be less amiable with each other, harsher, and they can use far more aggressive tactics to achieve what they desire. But in the second category, the manner in which the parties resolve their dispute is bound to have an important effect on their ongoing relationship and is very likely to determine whether they will be able to maintain an ongoing relationship. Therefore, their manner of dealing with each other during the dispute resolution process must be very different.

The root of the word *emotion* is from the Latin *e* "out" and *movere* "to move." Emotion is an energy passing through; it is the carrier wave upon which the person attaches his or her communication. Emotions may differ in quality one from another, and a particular emotion may be of greater or lesser intensity. That is why we use various words to describe the same emotion, according to the amplitude of the energy being expressed. There is a wide difference between rage or fury, on one hand, and annoyance or irritation, on the other, but both are a form of anger, expressed in different volumes.

A person may move from one emotion to another with great rapidity. For example, a person who is frightened, and whose desire therefore is to flee, may change and become angry, and the tendency of an angry person is to attack. If a person is too overwhelmed by the situation to be frightened or angry about it, she may fall into grief, in which state the energy is sitting huddled and is not moving one way or the other. In an extreme case of this, it turns into apathy, where the person is too numb even to feel the sensation of grief.

A person at rest may be, and usually is, in a different emotional state than when she starts communicating. The action of communicating requires energy, and that energy must be expressed in or through some kind of emotion. A common emotion is boredom, and boredom may be mild or acute. A person may feel intensely bored, experiencing it as a kind of pain, or simply mildly bored, resting, not doing very much, and this kind of boredom slides easily into a state of mild interest. Boredom is a condition in which the energy is not going anywhere; mild interest is a forward-moving emotion, which may turn into strong interest if stimulated, which is a strong outward-going energy, which in turn if stimulated may even turn into intense interest or even enthusiasm.

Feeling is synonymous with sensation, and the pursuit of most human beings is a pursuit for pleasant feelings and avoidance of unpleasant. "How are you feeling today?" "Oh, great." Feelings are entirely internal, when using the term *feeling* to describe a psychological state. Of course, one is subject to the stimuli of the senses, but such stimulation always gives rise to an internal feeling, and it is very difficult to say where that feeling resides or precisely what it consists of. But every person knows what it means to feel good, or feel bad, and there is such a wealth of subtle feelings that a human being is capable of experiencing that it may be said that human beings live through their experience of their own feelings.

All this is important for the mediator. Most people are apprehensive, which is a low-intensity fear, at the start of mediation. It is important that they become interested concerning the resolution of their conflict, because interest is the emotional energy they will need to reach the goal of resolution. Angry people simply want to attack, and furthermore the judgment of an angry person is usually impaired. However, sometimes people simulate anger to create an effect on their opponent without genuinely feeling that emotion themselves. It is natural that people enter mediation with apprehension, because they do not know if it is going to turn out the way they would wish. A mediator's job is to direct the parties' attention to the particular situation that requires resolution, and by getting them interested in the possibility of resolution, to bring them out of fear and anger into a state of interest in seeking resolution.

THIRTEEN

ANALYSIS AND HANDLING OF RISK

In real life you do not know the odds, you need discover them, and the sources of uncertainty are not defined.

(The Black Swan, Taleb, 2007)

The "haves," meaning the people with the money or the stuff, whatever it might be, tend to be loss averse. The "have-nots," meaning the people who want the money or the stuff, tend to be risk averse. Those who "have" need to conserve. Those who "have-not" need to acquire. Haves like to hang on to what they have. Have-nots are not free to take risks. This has implications for negotiation.

When a plaintiff makes a demand, it often might as well be monopoly money; it represents wishful thinking. When a defendant makes an offer, it is real money that the defendant would much prefer not to have to part with. Plaintiffs are hopeful; defendants are grudging. That is because, as we learn from behavioral economics, a person's sadness at losing $1,000 is twice as great as a person's joy at winning $1,000. This tendency to feel the pain of loss more deeply than the joy of gain is called "loss aversion" and affects the manner in which parties negotiate.

In Greek mythology, Sisyphus, king of Corinth, known for his cunning, managed to cheat Death—for a time. When he finally reached Hades for the second time, he was punished by having forever to roll a huge stone to the top of a hill, the stone always escaping him and rolling down again: perpetual labor. Negotiations can seem like that.

Defendants start at the bottom of the hill; with sighs and groans they explain how they just can't roll the stone—they are not liable, the plaintiff is a rogue, the case is only worth "nuisance value" at best, they refuse to be intimidated, the plaintiff will never be able to prove his case, the legal theories are flawed, and so on. Of course, defendants never reach the top of the hill because the top is whatever the plaintiff says it is, and plaintiffs like to dream.

Plaintiffs start at the top of the hill and energetically try to prevent the stone from rolling down. It may seem odd that the plaintiff gets to define the top of the hill, but this is a mythical hill, a metaphor—whatever the plaintiff selects as his opening demand is the top of the hill. A plaintiff with an injury worth around $15,000 may choose Mount Everest as his starting point: "The demand is $400,000." The penalty paid by a plaintiff for unrealistic expectations is that her stone is much harder to keep at or near the top because gravity, i.e., reality, pulls it down, and also his stone has farther to fall, which damages her credibility.

Gravity is the pull toward the natural resting place of the stone. The stone represents the "true" value of the case. A plaintiff may choose any number she pleases, but a defendant cannot fall lower than zero. Defendants always complain about this, gazing in amazement at the plaintiff's ball so high, so far away: "What's the point of negotiating at all?" they say. But defendants do not have to start at the bottom; they are allowed to start anywhere on the hill they choose. If they have to push the stone that much farther to find the stone's natural resting place, the choice was theirs.

The length and stress of a negotiation depends on how hard the parties want to work, how long they want to play, but even more depends on how close the parties are prepared to start negotiating somewhere in the vicinity of the natural resting place of the stone. They have an advantage that the mythical Sisyphus never had. Claims have a value within a certain range; the precise value can be determined only in hindsight.

RISK ANALYSIS

The gravity of a risk is its magnitude multiplied by its probability.

Russian roulette is a game in which a single bullet is placed in a revolver with six chambers. If you play this game, the chances are six to one in your favor. But the consequence of failure is death. Who would play the game for $5? $500? $5,000? $50,000? $500,000? $5,000,000? Some people would never play this game, no matter what the prize for survival, but others would find a point at which they are willing to take the risk.

If two bullets are placed in the revolver, the odds in favor of death have just doubled. Whoever plays the game now has only a three-in-one chance of survival. Not many people would accept such odds, but some will always be found who will take that chance if the rewards are enough, depending on their personal situation. People undergo operations for which the chance of a successful outcome is extremely low but for which the chance of survival without the operation is even lower. Some people are willing to kill themselves so their family can collect insurance proceeds.

People routinely wrongly assess the risk they are undertaking. Millions of people buy lottery tickets every week, which amounts to a kind of tax on their income, but they accept the exceedingly low odds of success because the amount at risk is merely the loss of the ticket price. But people will ruin themselves in casinos, where the odds are stacked against them yet are much better than the chances of winning a lottery, because their optimism keeps them believing that they are going to outwit "lady luck."

Human capacity to wreak destruction has increased by stunning orders of magnitude. Even with the immense risks involved, the Soviet Union and United States were prepared to play nuclear brinkmanship. Defense Secretary Robert McNamara rated the chance of all-out nuclear war during the peak years of the Cold War in the region of one in six. How many people would play Russian roulette with their own lives and a single bullet in the chamber? That is what we did as a nation.

As mediators, most of us are unlikely to hold the fate of millions of people in our hands, but the essential assessment of risk factors enters into play every time people engage in conflict, whether by way of litigation or otherwise. The disputants assess risk, consequence, and reward. They try to predict the likely outcome if they do not settle. Whether they do it instinctively or by laboriously examining every conceivable fact, they are estimating the magnitude of the risk multiplied by its probability and making their decisions accordingly. Very often, they get the equation wrong; in fact, looking at it purely statistically, whenever two parties got to war, or to trial, or escalate any conflict to the next step, one of them has misestimated the reality of the situation.

In any particular instance, it may be possible to estimate one's chances at greater or lesser than 50 percent, but over the long term the fifty-fifty proportion holds true.

In legal situations, if an attorney has a case with "weak liability," he may still take that case to trial if the potential payoff is very large. For example, if someone is involved in an automobile accident and rendered quadriplegic, then even if the chances of success are slim, many attorneys will take that chance because the injuries are so horrific that, if the jury finds in favor of the injured person, the compensation will be very large.

On the other hand, even where liability is considered a "slam dunk," a case may be settled for a relatively modest amount where the damages are quite low.

One of the main reasons that people settle their disputes is exhaustion rather than pessimism. People get into fights or lawsuits, and it is remarkable how optimistic both sides are about a favorable outcome. But these things have a tendency to drag on and on, and the longer they continue, the more likely it is that the disputants will simply get fed up with playing that particular game and wish to "move on with their lives." This is an important tool in the mediator's tool kit. Once the parties get involved in a conflict, it is as if they were dragging the burden behind them attached to one ankle by a rope. It slows them down. It takes their attention away from other things. What appeared at the beginning of the fight as being a most important principle may come to be seen over time as simply not worth all the bother.

Therefore, even though the assessment of risk may be entirely wrong, and even though parties may be unduly optimistic about their own chances, a time will come when they may be very ready to put the matter to bed.

When the mediator hears the words "I just want to get this over with," she knows that settlement is near at hand. People do stop fighting out of sheer exhaustion. So do nations.

Let him be rich and weary, that at least
If goodness lead him not, yet weariness
May toss him to my breast.

—George Herbert
(1593–1633)

FOURTEEN

NEGOTIATIONS WITHIN NEGOTIATION

If only two persons attend mediation and they both have authority to settle, then only three negotiations take place. They are between (1) person 1 and person 2, (2) person 1 and mediator, and (3) person 2 and mediator. The dynamics of this are easy to manage.

More commonly, at least four persons attend, namely, two parties and two attorneys, in which case ten dynamic interactions may take place, as follows: (1) party 1 and party 2, (2) party 1 and lawyer 1, (3) party 1 and mediator, (4) party 1 and lawyer 2, (5) party 2 and lawyer 2, (6) party 2 and mediator, (7) party 2 and lawyer 1, (8) lawyer 1 and mediator, (9) lawyer 2 and mediator, and (10) lawyer 1 and lawyer 2.

It is easy to draw a cat's cradle to demonstrate the complex dynamics that exist in the preceding simple mediation, with only two parties each represented by an attorney.

If this was a dinner party with five friends, the conversation would be a free-for-all with everyone having a wonderful time. But a mediator cannot afford to have a free-for-all in a mediation session. A mediation is a negotiation, and every negotiation is (however politely or amicably conducted) an adversarial process. Further, most mediations take place within a larger context of adversarial relationships, or adversarial process such as potential or pending litigation.

If there are multiple participants (i.e., more than two parties and two attorneys in a mediation), the cat's cradle becomes exponentially more complex—in fact, exceedingly complex. Such negotiations can easily get out of hand. It becomes all the more important for the mediator to set herself or himself as the focal point of all communications and to control cross-table communications quite carefully, with as much finesse as possible.

No one attends mediation without some kind of agenda. Every person's agenda is different.

The mediator must control the flow of communication or the negotiation will founder. That is why he was hired. With whatever subtlety or bluntness this is accomplished, it is essential. The mediator must be willing to shut off a destructive communication. He must also be willing to draw necessary communication out of participants who are keeping silent, even if this requires a private session.

The easiest way to control the dynamics of the situation, without attempting to stifle them, is to have the participants communicate with each other through the mediator. The slight deflection that this requires has an ameliorating effect on the language and the attitude of the speaker. As this is exactly what happens in court—attorneys are used to it.

There are only two kinds of communication in mediation. The first is any communication that keeps the negotiation moving toward clarity and settlement. The second is any communication that tends to torpedo, stifle, or impede clarity and settlement. When "bad" communications occur, as they always do, the mediator must repair the damage and move on.

There are only two venues for a communication. The first is in joint session. The second is in private session.

Joint sessions are for participants to communicate positively such facts, attitudes, interpretations, arguments, and offers as will tend to move the parties closer to the goal of settlement.

Individual sessions have two purposes. The first is to permit participants to "vent." Venting means to express negative thoughts and emotions about the other side. The setting in which such venting takes place must be controlled by the mediator in such a way as to advance, not impede, the purpose of settlement, and this means in private session. The purpose of venting is to get it said and done with. Some people take longer to vent than others. Some people never stop venting on their own volition, in which instance the mediator must make a calculated judgment when to call a halt to it. The second purpose of private session is to discuss what the participants will say in joint session, or what they want the mediator to convey to the other side.

Sometimes a participant wants to express his or her thoughts, emotions, feelings, or attitudes directly to the other side. This is the side of mediation that is closest to therapy. The only reason to permit this is if it will advance the settlement process. How this is done is very important. There is a world of difference between, on one hand, explaining how one feels and, on the other hand, engaging in a personal attack on another participant. This difference can be quite subtle. However much people are coached, sometimes they just cannot resist turning an account of how they feel into a personal attack. There is a simple rule concerning personal (ad hominem) attacks: Don't do it, however tempting, because it never helps and always makes things worse.

These issues do not always arise. Often, the volume and extent of these potentially explosive interactions is reduced or minimized by the parties themselves or their lawyers. Some lawyers prefer to keep their clients out of the negotiations, keeping them on hand to ratify settlement proposals. Some parties do not want to take an active part in the proceeding, feeling that is what they retained an attorney to do for them. Also, attorneys often do not want their clients interacting directly with the other side's attorney. Some clients become terribly frustrated with the other side's attorney, seeing him or her as the supreme obstacle—sometimes such a client takes the opportunity to call the other side's attorney a liar; the mediator should put a stop to such fighting words because they will wreck the negotiation.

FIFTEEN

ANALYTICAL VERSUS INTUITIVE THINKING

A nalytical and intuitive thinking are not the same; each has strengths and weaknesses, and the two combined may be called *holistic thinking*. Because "thinking" is in its nature invisible and abstract, it may be helpful to use an analogy by way of representation: the anatomy of the cornea.

At the center of the cornea are clustered cone cells, which have the function of focusing on objects far or near. Surrounding the cone cells are more numerous rod cells, which provide peripheral vision. If the cone cells deteriorate, when one attempts to focus upon an object, it disappears; a black spot in the center. But if you lose peripheral vision, even if you retain the ability to focus, it is like observing the world one speck at a time through the means of the focused beam of a flashlight. It is much easier to get around with only peripheral vision than with only focused vision.

This analogy can be convincing when seeking to demonstrate that analysis is not the whole universe of thinking. Law schools, for example, specialize in teaching analytical thinking and may tend to dismiss intuition as "touchy-feely." That term betrays unawareness of the fact that just as the cone cells are surrounded by more numerous rod cells, so the penetrative power of analytical thinking is made possible only by the provision of context afforded by the intuitive. If you have no intuition of where to look, you cannot focus the concentrated beam of analysis at the right target.

Analytical thinking is historically quite recent, whereas intuitive thinking has been mankind's chief possession since the dawn of time. As far as Western civilization is concerned, the classical Greeks "invented" analytical thinking; the Romans built really straight roads with it, the Dark Ages lost it, and the Enlightenment rediscovered it. We can partly attribute the triumphs and perils of our modern civilization to the relative imbalance in the importance afforded to analytical versus intuitive skills over the last four hundred years. The current dysfunction of the legal system is also in part a consequence of this imbalance. The broad mission of mediation may be to restore the balance, because we are now in a time when the perils threaten to outweigh the triumphs. Overly analytical people are to a large extent "blind"; our society needs people who can "think" with a whole eye, which is called holistic thinking—only those who are out of touch with feeling call this "touchy-feely."

Analytical thinking is powerful. It is focused, sharp, and linear; deals with one thing at a time; contains time; is deconstructive; contains no perspective; is subject to disorientation; is brain centered; and tends to the abstract. Analytical thinking is efficient in the following conditions—sufficient time, relatively static conditions, a clear differentiation between the observer and the observed. It is best suited for dealing with complexities and works best where there are established criteria for the analysis (e.g., rules of law). It is necessary when an explanation is required, seeks the best option, and can be taught in the classroom to beginners.

Intuitive thinking has contrasting qualities: It is unfocused, nonlinear, contains "no time," sees many things at once, views the big picture, contains perspective, is heart centered, is oriented in space and time, and tends to the real or concrete. Intuition comes into its own where analytical thinking is inadequate: under time pressure, where conditions are dynamic, where the differentiation between observer and observed is unclear. It works best where the observer has experience in the particular situation, is difficult to teach in the classroom, eschews seeking the "best" option in favor of the "workable," and is prepared to act on feelings or hunches where either explanations are not required or there is no time for them. Intuition is experience translated by expertise to produce rapid action.

Intuition is limited where the task is complex and uncertain, where the observer lacks experience, or the observation is distorted by biases or fixed ideas. Its weakness is a tendency to produce a fixed attitude or mind-set that ignores new data; that is why the analytical thinking of the Enlightenment was so revolutionary. Intuition is ineffective for predicting the stock market, or for discovering that the heart is a pump, or for dissecting a legal problem.

When analytical and intuitive abilities are combined, the result is "holistic." To effect settlements and resolutions, it is necessary to move people out of a rights/obligations/win–lose mind-set into a needs/interests/mutual gain mind-set, which is what mediation is all about—this requires holistic thinking abilities.

"The intuitive mind is a sacred gift and the rational mind is a faithful servant. We have created a society that honors the servant and has forgotten the gift."

—attributed to Albert Einstein

TABLE OF COMPARISON	
ANALYTICAL	**INTUITIVE**
Time	No time
Static	Dynamic
Linear	Nonlinear
One thing	Many things
Small picture	Big picture
Focused	Nonfocused
Deliberative	Instantaneous
No perspective	Perspective
Classroom taught	Experience taught
Objective	Subjective
Best option	Workable option
Explanation required	Action required
Deconstructive	Constructive
Object differentiation	Pattern matching

Objective / subjective	No clear objective / subjective
Brain centered	Heart centered
Disoriented	Oriented
Abstract	Concrete
Historically new	Historically old
Lawyers	Firefighters

SIXTEEN

THE OCTAVE OF EMOTIONS

Apathy, Sadness, Fear, Anger, Boredom,
Interest, Enthusiasm, Elation

Negotiators are sometimes taught that emotion is preferably avoided. Just as the legal system goes to considerable lengths to keep emotional expression out of courtrooms many of the popular books on negotiation and mediation barely discuss the emotions at all, other than to focus on methods to "deal with" emotions should they intrude. They treat emotion as something that gets in the way of problem solving. The closest they get is to divide emotions into "positive or negative." The list of "positives" are mostly synonyms, and the reader is then directed what to do with any "negatives," such as take a deep breath, count to ten, work out an analytical response and so on.

This presents a perspective that emotion is integral to all forms of human interaction, indeed integral to any communication, even with corporations that are just fictional or "legal" entities. It implies that we tend as a society to suffer not from excess but from deficit of emotional expression. It suggests that a good deal of social interaction today is inclined to exhibit a "flat affect," characterized as "severe reduction in emotional expressiveness, speaking in a monotonous voice, having diminished facial expressions." The difficulty in negotiation and mediation is not too much emotion but either too little or hiding in disguise, so the negotiators and the mediator must be able to read signs, clues, and "tells" to understand what is going on beneath veneers of rationality.

If we talk only in terms of positive and negative emotions, we are shortchanging ourselves and precluding understanding. Emotion needs to be perceived as the movement of energy, which is neither positive nor negative but merely a response to a situation. The different emotions are evolutionary responses to environmental factors. One reason human emotion can seem complicated is because we have memories, and not only our own memories but the memories of others that can carry an emotional charge for us; one can also feel conflicting emotions, meaning several emotions simultaneously. One can also be moved emotionally by works of fiction or stories from the past.

An emotion may be acute or chronic. Children's emotions tend to be acute, flaring and fading as the child moves from one emotion to another; the emotion is fluid. But a person may become so habituated to a given emotional response that it becomes chronic; the emotion is stuck. An abused child may become chronically apathetic or fearful. We can find in mediation that a person is unreasonably or inexplicably angry, and we cannot tell where the anger is coming from because there does not appear to be any immediate stimulus for it. The answer may be that the person is stuck in a particular emotion as a chronic response to life. This is emotional constipation; releasing it can be daunting.

Normal children are easily excited; they rush at life. But it is not uncommon to come across adults who seldom smile and for whom a mild interest is about as intense an emotion as they are able to feel. The vibrant societies of the past have been full of conflict, yet buzzing with enthusiasm and excitement for projects upon which we now gaze in wonder and amazement. That is why so many people visit Florence, where the architecture is testimony to an explosion of artistic energy expressed as intense appetite for life; yet Florence was notorious for civil strife and murderous conflict as well as artistic genius.

Emotion means what the word suggests; it is an energetic expression of movement. Without emotion, no one would get out of bed in the morning, and some people don't. Emotion is the wellspring of action. Dividing emotions into just two categories, positive and negative, is highly simplistic. As soon as one recognizes that emotion is an expression of energy, it becomes easy to comprehend because we know a lot about other forms of energy.

An analogy is with music, where the energy of a sound expressed as a wavelength has been exhaustively studied. A single note is a form of energy emitted as a wave, which is received and interpreted as a particular sound. Emotions can be viewed the same way. Every note contains qualities, such as volume, duration, frequency or pitch, and timbre, so that a single note can be expressed in a number of different ways. Western music divides notes into octaves consisting of eight major notes and any number of minor notes between them, and each octave has one above it and one below it, ad infinitum. The note expressed in one octave may be repeated in a higher or lower octave.

Harmonics are created by combining different notes. Many sounds are way beyond our human range: "Astronomers have detected the deepest note ever generated in the cosmos, a B-flat flying through space like a ripple on an invisible pond... 57 octaves below the keys in the middle of a piano." Perhaps emotions are also infinite, but we lack the sensory organs to perceive more than a few.

Some emotions propel us forward. Some emotions propel us backward. Some emotions propel us inward. Emotions are an expression of direction, and the impulse to move in a direction.

Emotions are neither positive nor negative, which is merely to overlay a given emotion with a value judgment, but are developed evolutionary responses to environmental stimuli. The worst thing that can be said about an emotion is that it may be inappropriate to the present situation, and this arises as a function of time and memory, because past emotions may be carried forward in time. But no emotion is inherently negative. Writers on the subject are apt to label fear and anger as negative, but in certain circumstances fear or anger are the exactly appropriate emotions. All emotional response is designed to protect the integrity of the individual organism. Fleeing in panic may well save your life, and occasionally we read heartwarming press accounts of tiny 90-year-old ladies swinging their handbags or walking sticks to beat off young thugs.

The primary emotions are sometimes described as sad, mad, glad, and scared; this rhymes nicely but is incomplete. We need some more to get an octave of eight primary emotions. These are the do, ra, me, fa, so, la, ti, do of emotions—apathy, sadness, fear, anger, boredom, interest, enthusiasm, and elation. The octave expresses the movement of energy in sequence, and such movement is in a given direction.

Apathy. The octave of primary emotions starts with apathy, an emotion intensely unpleasant to experience and in which one would expect the actor to make attempts to dull the pain of that dark, inward-looking, sludgy, unmoving congealed emotion. Here we might find substance abusers, because substance abuse is a response to pain and apathy is experienced as pain. Apathy is what happens if grief is continued too long. When the tears have stopped pumping but the situation has not improved, then a person may sink into a low state of almost no energy manifesting at all. The person is not outward looking, and has ceased to be inward looking, but is merely sitting miserably. This may be considered close to pathological. Apathy looks nowhere, sad looks inward, scared looks around for refuge, mad looks around for a target, boredom looks around distractedly, interest looks around with focus, enthusiasm looks around with passion, and elation looks nowhere in particular but feels wonderful. Between these primary emotional "notes" we can find half notes, quarter notes, and so forth, until it becomes no longer useful to categorize.

If one can help that person to move out of that awful condition, they might be able to experience an outpouring of grief for the frightfulness of their condition or past events that brought them to that condition. We see that such a change in emotion is a large step forward, as the movement of the energy goes from almost no movement at all to an outpouring, a pumping of energy literally expressed by the body as tears. Such catharsis brings a great sense of relief.

Grief. The "note" of grief (sadness) may vary in volume, pitch, intensity, and timbre, and then we use different descriptions such as misery, sorrow, anguish, desolation, or heartache. The low-intensity note of fear may be called concern, anxiety, or apprehension; a high volume of fear may be called terror or panic.

While fear deals with threatened loss, grief deals with actual loss. Grief is an inward-looking emotion; its outward manifestation is tears. It is unhelpful to say to a person who is grieving, "There, there, don't cry." It is better to encourage the tears, or at least do nothing to stifle them. Grief is a natural and evolutionary response to loss. It is also called sadness. The flow of tears may be likened to a ritual washing or cleansing, a washing away of the wound. Grief lasts as long as it lasts and, when it is over, the person is then ready to reemerge into the world. In traditional societies, a grieving person is often secluded during the period of mourning, in order to permit the attention of the organism to focus on the process of healing. It is uncomfortable for a grieving person to focus on business or worldly affairs. That is why, after the terrorist attacks on New York's Twin Towers on September 11, 2001, it was difficult in many instances to persuade the loved ones of those killed to file claims for compensation, even though the deadline was fast approaching, because they had not yet completed the grieving process and were therefore not yet ready to get on with their lives.

Fear. Fear is a more active expression of energy than grief because fear wants to propel the organism in a particular direction, away from the perceived threat; it is a flight mechanism. Flight not only requires more in the way of hormonal activation but is more survival oriented than sitting in a puddle of tears. There is nothing wrong with tears or grief, but in that condition, the organism is more vulnerable to attack. When one is in headlong flight, one has a better chance of survival. Fear results in, or is an expression of, the release of adrenalin, because both anger and fear require movement and adrenalin charges the muscles, the difference being that the movement is in opposite directions. The intensity of fear can be so great as to produce paralysis instead of flight, and intense anger can be equally dangerous, inducing apoplexy.

Anger. As a matter of a slight switch in direction, the adrenalin-charged muscles that are propelling the organism in headlong flight may turn into the forward emotion of attack. Thus, fear can turn into anger, but anger lacks judgment and is therefore risky. Anger has a bad reputation in our society because it is potentially dangerous, and furthermore its source may lie in the past, invisible to an observer and perhaps inaccessible to the person experiencing it. We see this most commonly with people who get upset and angry over what seem like trifles. We are talking to a person and suddenly something we say triggers an anger response. This can be quite confusing because the person experiencing the anger focuses on the triviality, being unaware of the underlying cause. This creates an impasse because the trigger for the anger seemed insignificant to anyone observing it.

The reason people fear anger is that anger is the emotion of forward attack. Faced with an expression of anger, the potential recipient is faced with an immediate decision, whether to flee the scene, whether to appease, whether to submit, whether to counterattack. All these options must be processed at a lightning speed without much analytical input, which in turn creates stress, manifested in the body as the release of adrenalin and other hormonal responses. An angry person lacks good judgment; that is why lawyers try to induce anger in their opponents or opposing witnesses—so they will make a mistake.

Anger is directed outward, and it sees the environment as a threat. It is not cowed, but it lacks judgment and is apt to take risks in an effort to overcome the threat. So it is not a useful emotion for the calm resolution of problems, but it is fairly close in terms of energetic wavelength to achieving a state of interest, which is the desired state for problem-solving. In 1987, the author Joyce Carol Oates said something interesting about anger: "In any case, anger is an appropriate response to certain intransigent facts of life, not a motiveless malignancy as in classic tragedy but a fully motivated and socially coherent impulse."

The low-intensity note of anger may be called irritability, annoyance, or aggravation; high-volume anger may be called rage or fury. The anger of a psychopath (*Silence of the Lambs movie*) is not the same as the anger of a child (*Kramer vs. Kramer movie*), which is not the same as the anger of a fighter (*Rocky movie*), which is not the same as the anger of a writer, and so on, in all the situations of life.

Boredom. Beyond anger there is boredom, and many people act bored whether as a tactic or genuinely, but boredom is not far from interest, and interest is where we want to be. Boredom may be chronic or acute; it may be felt as dull pain or with exquisite intensity. Notice that whereas grief was not going anywhere energetically, fear was going backward and anger was going forward, boredom is not going anywhere but is distracted and looking around, and interest is moving forward. We want the energy to move in a forward direction outward toward the particular situation or problem that needs to be resolved; we want at some point to be able to apply analytical skills.

Whereas grief lies close to fear, boredom lies between anger and interest. Boredom is an emotion associated with feelings of discomfort, distractedness, of looking around for something to do and not finding it. Whereas grief is active but looks inward, boredom is also active but looks outward; it is not really moving, but it would like to be moving. Boredom is quite a good place to be because it is not hard to pass quickly from boredom to interest. This is readily observable in children, hanging around the house whining, "There's nothing to do," but as soon as something is promised—a trip to the playground, a new game to play, a friend to play with—a child can snap instantly from boredom to excitement. Young children move freely from one emotion to another, as long as they have not been abused. Some people are wholly and totally fed up with their jobs; they experience boredom as a chronic condition, and it is painful.

Interest. The desirable emotion for parties in negotiation, and indeed in life, is interest. Parties may start the process apathetic about the outcome, grieving about their loss, fearful of the outcome, angry with the opponent, or resentful about being there at all. These emotions are not inappropriate but need to be worked on so that, over time, the parties will come to be interested in resolving the particular situation in which they find themselves. Interest may be mild or intense; if it becomes very intense it may change pitch and become elation or enthusiasm.

Interest is the emotion at which analytical problem-solving processes become available. That is why it is sometimes not recognized as an emotion at all, but when one realizes that the development of analytical thinking led to a massive and sustained outpouring of investigation into every aspect of existence, it is easy to see the kind of emotional energy that interest represents. It is outgoing, forward-looking, and engaged. Interest is the point at which life can be lived. The word comes from the Latin: *inter* 'between' and *esse* 'to be'; it is the quality of energy at which one can emerge from one's isolation and notice that one is not alone.

Elation. Beyond intense interest is enthusiasm. Enthusiasm means literally "possession by a god," and elation or joy is what happens to enthusiasm when it is considerably heightened. We don't see this in negotiation or mediation too much, but for those purposes, interest is good enough. Excitement is similar to elation but expresses different pitch and timbre.

Elation may turn into pure joy, which is what the Romantic poets wrote about:

Hail to thee, blithe Spirit! Bird thou never wert,
That from heaven, or near it, Pourest thy full heart
In profuse strains of unpremeditated art.

—"To a Skylark," Shelley

Participants come to a negotiation carrying with them the burden and stress not only of the conflict itself but also of the underlying situation that caused the conflict in the first place. The accumulation of wounds that occupies so much of their attention lies in the past, yet clearly the resolution of the problem lies in the future. The problem arrives encrusted with baggage of unexpressed emotions, with pain; bitterness and despair; or anger, frustration, and apprehension. These things need to be addressed to liberate attention sufficiently to permit participants to concentrate on the future. In this sense, mediation is a process of moving a person's attention from the past to the future. Similarly, the octave of emotions tends to move from the past (apathy, grief) to an uncomfortable present (fear, anger, boredom) to a lively anticipated future (interest, enthusiasm, elation). If that is accomplished, then it is possible to leave the past behind along with all its accumulated baggage, and this achievement is accompanied by a feeling of relief. Participating in this feeling is one reason why mediators like their job.

SEVENTEEN

THE DYNAMICS OF MEDIATED NEGOTIATION

T he term *dynamics* refers to the motivating or driving forces, the action of forces, motion and equilibrium, growth, change, and development. The relationship between human beings is dynamic rather than static.

In mediation, each individual in the room is necessarily involved in several simultaneous relationships, which are divisible into two broad categories. First, every person has his or her own relationship with the subject matter of the dispute itself. In a breach of contract dispute, a party has his or her own feelings about the contract, what it meant in terms of benefits, future profits, security, an increase in business, a vacation in Italy, an extension on the house, whatever it might represent to that person.

The retained attorney has quite a different relationship to the subject matter, viewing it through the very particular lens of legal reasoning, the elements of the contractual relationship, the evidence that will be required, and the amount of damages that can be established. Each party, and each lawyer, will have a different viewpoint or perspective of the dispute's subject matter.

Reconciling these viewpoints sufficiently to reach a satisfactory closure is the delicate task of the mediator. But don't expect one party to come bouncing out of his corner explaining to the other, "Of course, I see it now; you were right all along," or one party to fall sobbing into the arms of the other—not impossible but unlikely. The resolution is usually just enough to achieve closure of the particular dispute; that is often enough for the participants, and if the mediator can facilitate that outcome, she can count it as a job well done.

In addition to the dynamic relationship of each participant with the dispute's subject matter, each also has some kind of relationship with all the other participants. When we talk about dynamics in relationship to two people, we are generally referring to the energetic qualities of the relationship between them. When we talk about the dynamics of mediation, we are referring to the set of relationships that come together specifically for the purpose of the mediation.

The minimum number of persons attending any mediation is three. The two disputants have already established a relationship, and it is unlikely to be a comfortable or easy relationship, otherwise they would not be in mediation seeking assistance to resolve their conflicts. That relationship, though it may be troubled and even hostile, is nevertheless a strong bond between those two people; if it were not a strong connection, they would be able to dissolve it by their own efforts. For some reason, or for a series of reasons, they are unable to disentangle themselves on their own. They come to a mediator for assistance.

The connection between the mediator and each party is a temporary and relatively weak connection. Nonetheless, the mediator's relationship with the parties is important, at least for the duration of the negotiation. The mediator must develop a relationship of trust and confidence, and if possible of some influence and authority, during the course of the mediation.

The mediator is often the person who must take responsibility for bringing the matter to mutually satisfactory closure. In many instances, the parties may make some headway, but the pattern of their relationship is such that they cannot take the decisive concluding steps.

In the simplest of all mediations, as far as the complexity of dynamics is concerned, it is easy to see that there are only three relationships involved: the mediator with each of the parties, and the parties with each other.

All mediations occurring in the context of litigation have five persons at least in the mediation session; two lawyers, two parties, and the mediator. It is easy to see that the number of relationships has just doubled. Each lawyer has a relationship with his or her own client. Each lawyer has a relationship of some sort with the other lawyer. The clients have a relationship with each other. In addition, the mediator has a relationship with each opponent, considering the opponent consists of the party and his attorney. That makes six. If the number of people in the mediation increases—for example, in a multiparty mediation—then the complex dynamics of the relationship in the room increases accordingly.

The job of the mediator is to manage the dynamics in the room. To manage them, she has to be sensitive to them. The way to be sensitive to the dynamics is to be aware of them, meaning consciously to observe what is going on between the various parties in the room. Sometimes their attitudes toward each other will be muted, and therefore more difficult to discern. At other times they will be open with each other, even if they are angry or hostile toward each other.

Going into the mediation, the mediator has no idea what the particular dynamics of the mediation are going to look like. She can be reasonably confident that the mediation is going to be different in some way or another from every other mediation. A mediator must be alert and aware to assess the dynamics in the room and to make the various decisions that she has to make, that is to say, whether to split the parties into private session, whether to keep them in joint session, who to speak to first, whether to attempt to address a party directly or only through his attorney, and so on.

The mediator has no time to weigh up these decisions. She must "go with the gut," trusting to one's instinct the immediate decision. To do this effectively, it is a good idea to practice observing and sensing the dynamics in the room in order to make the decision that will move the process in the speediest and most effective manner.

As an example, two specialized retailers of a rare and expensive com-modity got into a dispute. These two intelligent people, who knew each other well, were both angry, and after a while it was evident that their lawyers felt uneasy with the level of anger that they were exhibiting toward each other. The mediator made the decision to put the two litigants in the room together without their attorneys. It is not easy to get an attorney to agree to part with the client during mediation, because clients retain attor-neys for the specific purpose of representing them, but in this instance they both agreed. That is an achievement of the mediator requiring diplomacy as well as willingness to risk failure The mediator sat in the room with the two while they yelled at each other for half an hour, exchanging arguments and abuse at a high pitch. When they had concluded their yelling match, they arrived at a conclusion satisfactory to both of them. They got up, shook hands, and immediately started doing business with each other. That is an example of a certain dynamic at work. The mediator took the risk of blowing the negotiation sky-high but had observed that those two had a certain way of dealing with each other—tough negotiators, not afraid of expressing emotion, but smart—and the moment was ripe, because they couldn't have talked this way to each other before this moment.

"Ripeness is all."

—*King Lear,*
Shakespeare

Let us consider further the dynamics that are present in mediation. It has already been stated that the first relationship to be considered is the relationship of the individual with the event itself. Then the reaction of the individual to the event is an important factor to consider in resolution of the dispute.

DIFFERENT TYPES OF DISPUTE

A **vehicle accident** occurs when two vehicles try to occupy the same space at the same time. The purpose of every auto accident case is to determine which driver had the legal right to occupy that space; once that is determined, it must follow that the driver who did not have the right to occupy the space is at fault for the accident.

In **employment cases**, when a person is passed over for a promotion, it is because another person was chosen to occupy that particular position or space. The aggrieved person may seek to find some legal grounds for blaming the employer, for example, discrimination on gender, racial, age, or other unlawful grounds for choosing one person over another.

In **real estate matters**, people get into boundary disputes with their neighbors. Or a dispute arises because of an overhanging tree branch, or a barking dog, or a garbage bin, or an intruding tree root—always some alleged intrusion. Sometimes a person complains that the branch of a tree owned by the city breaks off and strikes a vehicle. That is the case of the branch and the automobile trying to occupy the same space at the same time.

Intentional acts, which are called *intentional torts*, do not fall into the neat formulation of "same space, same time" or "reaching for the same thing at the same time." An intentional tort may be a defamation, for example, in which the injured person alleges that someone has deliberately put about a false statement to damage his reputation—this is a case of the attempted displacement of a person's reputation with another, false reputation. Or when someone attacks another person in a bar. Or shoots them, which is a case of a bullet displacing the space occupied by a body part. A breach of contract case occurs when one party alleges that the other party promised to do something and failed to perform as promised. Or promised to refrain from doing something but then went ahead and did it.

Disputes may fall into a great variety of legal categories. Here are some examples: business and corporate, civil rights, construction defect, breach of contract, violation of law regarding senior citizens, employment discrimination, employment harassment, employment termination, entertainment (which is generally a specialized case of contract breach), environmental, family matters including divorce and care of children, fraud, home owners association disputes, insurance coverage, intellectual property including copyright, trademarks and patents, labor relations, legal malpractice, medical malpractice, partnership disputes, automobile accidents, other accidents, accidents on private or public property, probate and trust disputes, liability for defective products, real property disputes, toxic torts, and unfair competition.

SUBJECTIVE AND OBJECTIVE ASPECTS OF EVERY DISPUTE

The objective situation consists of the facts, as best as they can be ascertained, and often include the legal framework into which those facts need to be fitted. The subjective aspects consist of the individual's reaction to that external or objective situation. The mediator must consider both.

Then, separately considered, is the relationship between the parties to the dispute, very often two parties but not infrequently a number of different parties. The parties develop a relationship with each other. It may be unwilling, very often it is not cordial, but it exists nonetheless, and it is often remarkably difficult to disentangle the parties from each other, even though each of them have perspectives that are likely to be entirely different. A characteristic of nearly all disputes is that the people involved blame each other for the mess they are in. It is rare—in fact, it never happens—that a party comes to a mediated dispute that has been going on for a while in a mood to accept complete responsibility.

THE MEDIATOR MUST CONSIDER MANY PERSPECTIVES

Before coming to mediation, the methods that people have used to attempt to resolve the situation have, as often as not, made matters worse, and certainly more expensive. So the question for the mediator to ask himself is, "What is the relationship?" This question requires one or more adjectives in response. The mediator is looking for a description of the relationship of the party with the objective situation. Is it rational or irrational? Is the relationship cynical, or outraged, or purely monetary, or very upset, or mildly upset, or merely wishing to put things right, or completely one-sided, or able to see to some extent both sides of the situation, or interested, or somewhat bored, or frightened, or angry? It should be possible for the mediator to come to a determination, even if tentative, as to the relationship of the party with the objective situation, which is perhaps just another way of saying, "What are his feelings about or toward what he is going through?"

Next to be considered is the relationship of the party with the other party—or, if there are numerous people involved, with each one of them separately. Sometimes when people get into a dispute, they are very polite to each other and do nothing to make the situation worse. For example, there is a wide variation in how insurance company agents respond to a claim; and how they respond can ease matters, or exacerbate them, resulting in litigation when none was needed.

Often, a person will say to the mediator, "I only wanted to get my vehicle taken care of, but they jerked me around so badly that now I want to get my full measure of damages." Neighbors can get into a conflict with each other over matters such as barking dogs, or using each other's trash cans, or overhanging tree branches, or loud music, and what began as a relatively trifling matter that could have been resolved by some accommodation on the part of one of them, or both, may turn into a full-blown lawsuit. If that happens, then the parties will get involved in new relationships, between themselves and their attorneys and between themselves and their bank balances. Often people come into mediation having already spent far more than the matter was worth in the first place.

Leaving aside the question of whether they have been well served by their attorneys, they now have the problem of what are called "sunk costs," which are the costs that they have already spent. This adds an entirely new dimension to the possibility of resolution, because each side wants to get its money back. So, one often finds that a single problem has morphed into two problems: the original barking dog, now coupled with $18,000 in sunk costs. Sunk costs are costs that will never be recovered.

DIFFERING AGENDAS

Not only does a person develop a relationship with his attorney, which also may be characterized in different ways, such as respectful, cordial, trusting, upset, not consulted, too expensive, untrustworthy, put my trust fully in her, and so on, but also the attorney's agenda is not necessarily the same as the client's. For many clients, this may be their one and only contact with an attorney, and even if they are sophisticated in the matter of attorneys and the use of attorneys, every client is to every attorney as every car buyer is to every car salesman. That is to say, the attorney does it all the time and has numerous clients. Even if you buy a new car once a year, you are dealing with a car salesman who sells three cars a week; the car salesman knows a lot more about it than you ever will, and has a different agenda. The attorney of course is ethically bound to advance his client's best interests, and certainly many attorneys are conscientious in this regard, but necessarily the client's perspective on the matter will be different from the attorney's, and the dynamic relationship between the client and the attorney must be observed carefully by the mediator.

In particular, in any mediation, the mediator's aim is to get the parties to cooperate in seeking a resolution to the situation, whereas previously they had been competing to try to defeat each other. During the course of mediation, it is nearly always the case that, of the people in the room, some are willing to cooperate in the process, whereas some are impeding progress toward resolution, whether they are doing this deliberately or reactively, consciously or somewhat unconsciously. The mediator must learn how to notice who is holding things up, because that is the person who needs to be explored further. Then there is the relationship between the two attorneys, or between the many attorneys in the room, each with the other to the extent that they have developed a relationship. Sometimes those relationships are professional and cooperative. Sometimes they have been exacerbated, and the attorneys are upset with each other, and in such instances it is important for the mediator to realize that the relationship between the attorneys is itself a potential impediment to the resolution of the matter.

Finally, these relationships may be fairly weak, but quite often they will be strong and intense. By the time matters get into mediation, they have often been in conflict quite a while and the parties have become entangled with each other. Perceptions have changed over time, and attitudes may have hardened because of real or imagined slights or insults along the way. If attorneys are involved, they may have gotten under each other's skin, and the clients are nearly always painfully aware of the amount of money they have already spent, which they are dragging behind them in the form of sunk costs, often irrecoverable.

Each person in the room will have a different perception of the mediator, and the relationship of each person, including the attorneys, with the mediator is bound to be a relatively weak connection, because the relationship is temporary and often no one has ever met the mediator before. Part of the vital task of the mediator is to develop a relationship of trust and confidence on the part of the parties and their advisors in the mediator so that they have sufficient appreciation of his abilities to allow him to make his influence come to bear in assisting them in resolving the dispute.

You must have more than an intellectual understanding of suffering, its causes, and the antidotes; you must practice for this understanding to mature... Once you have gained this realization, you become as fearless and powerful as a snow lion. You have then achieved the state of confidence... you are now fully capable of serving others' needs.

—A Spacious Path to Freedom
(Karma Chagme)

EIGHTEEN

CONVENING

Negotiation consists of five stages: Convening, Opening,
Communicating, Negotiating, and Closing.

The first stage of a negotiation or mediated negotiation is called *convening.*

Convene derives from the Latin *con* 'with' and *venire* 'to come'—to come together.

A number of preliminary issues need to be addressed, as part of the convening process: (1) Who will serve as mediator? (2) Will the mediation be confidential? (3) What is the scope of the issues to be addressed? (4) Who will attend the mediation? (5) Where will the mediation be held?

In selecting a mediator, parties are looking for someone whom they believe is knowledgeable about the process, who understands or is able to understand the particular issues of the dispute, and who is perceived as impartial.

It is common practice for participants to share the expenses of the mediation. Sometimes, however, one party may agree to pay all or a larger share of that expense. That itself is a matter of negotiation between the parties. Generally, however, the expense of mediation is shared equally.

Mediations are conducted privately; only participants may attend. It is not a public hearing and, in most jurisdictions in which mediation has become established, the mediation itself is subject to confidentiality rules.

It used to be that mediators would themselves have a standard confidentiality agreement, or an agreement would be reached between the parties themselves, but in many jurisdictions today the confidentiality of settlement negotiations is written into law, and the mediation is nothing more or less than a mediated settlement negotiation protected by statute.

In such jurisdictions, mediations are confidential, to the extent permitted by law, even though some mediators may also use a confidentially agreement. However, where there is legislation in place, there is a potential risk in drafting a confidentiality agreement if it departs, being either more or less extensive in its terms, from the confidentiality law itself. If a confidentiality agreement falls short of the protections provided by law, is the agreement vitiated to the extent that it fails to provide protections already in statute, or would the courts hold that the parties themselves had waived the protections of the statute? Or, if the mediation agreement provides for a greater degree of confidentially than provided by law and is challenged by a third party, will the parties be allowed to keep confidential the matters that the law states are not to be kept confidential?

Parties or attorneys sometimes want to know whether the mediator wants to be "briefed" in advance and, if so, to what extent. The mediator should not seek to know all that the participants know; it is impossible, and it is unnecessary. Her skills lie elsewhere, and having one other person learn the entire story is not the best way to add value. A two- to four-page letter is usually sufficient to describe the nature of the dispute and is preferable to spending half an hour at the start of the mediation educating the mediator.

Once the parties have agreed to mediate, the most important consideration is that all persons with settlement authority actually show up for the mediation. A telephone "appearance" is usually insufficient. Nonetheless, it is quite common, where spouses are concerned, for only one spouse to appear with authority to negotiate for both of them. It is important to show up.

"Eighty percent of success is showing up."

—attributed to Groucho Marx and others

NINETEEN
OPENING

O nce the parties and their advisors, if any, have arrived, the next step is to begin the mediation. This is called "the opening." This is an important moment, and as we learn from an impeccable source, beginnings are not always easy:

Pooh looked at his two paws. He knew that one of them was the right, and he knew that when you had decided which one of them was the right, then the other one was the left, but he could never remember how to begin.

—A. A. Milne,
The House at Pooh Corner

T he mediator has to figure out how to begin. Many textbook writers consider that the mediator should make an opening statement, though many mediators do not make an opening statement at all but simply start the conversation. In his well-known textbook *The Mediation Process*, Christopher W. Moore identifies eleven topics to be addressed by the mediator in the opening statement:

1. Introduction of the mediator, and if appropriate, the parties.

2. Commendation of the willingness of the parties to cooperate and seek a solution to their problems.

3. Definition of mediation and the mediator's role.

4. Statement of impartiality and neutrality.

5. Description of mediation procedures.

6. Explanation of the concept of the caucus.

7. Definition of the parameters of confidentiality.

8. Description of logistics.

9. Suggestions for behavioral guidelines.

10. Answering questions posed by the parties.

11. Joint commitment to begin.

The initial decision for the mediator is whether to make an opening statement at all. Often, mediation is conducted in the presence of attorneys, who have been through the process many times before and who have already explained to their clients what is going to happen. In these situations, it is not necessary for the mediator to make a long speech. Even if the mediator wanted to, she is not going to get the parties to relax; they are not there to relax, they are there to resolve a situation. They are there to work.

The mediator cannot establish an atmosphere of trust, confidence, and safety just by making a little speech at the outset. If she does her job correctly, the parties will develop trust and confidence in the mediator and feel safe in confiding in her, but this is a task to be accomplished over time, sometimes many hours. If the parties are going to accomplish what they came for, they will need to keep all their attention focused on their conflict and the means of resolving it, and it is not necessarily going to be comfortable, or even feel all that safe, for them to make the moves they are going to have to make in order to achieve resolution. Furthermore, they are going to have to make difficult choices during the mediation, weighing different options, including the option of escalating the conflict. Mediation is intended to produce a result. It is not necessarily a pleasant and comfortable process to go through. Maybe it's more like having a tooth pulled—horrible, but great relief when it's over.

Some people really do choose continued conflict in preference to the challenge and the pain of communicating with each other. Indeed, parties may become embroiled in conflict, get into litigation, and proceed all the way through a trial without ever having to communicate with each other, without ever having to make any concession, without ever having to change their minds about anything or alter any position. They may prefer this option. Some people prefer to fight and will not have it any other way.

"What, [sword] drawn and talk of peace! I hate the word".

—Shakespeare,
Romeo & Juliet

Conflict may be the more comfortable option; it may seem less confrontational than talking. As one well-known mediator put it, "Mediation is not for sissies." However, the mediator has to make a choice. Obviously, the first thing the mediator does is to introduce himself to the parties, one at a time, and to their attorneys or advisors, if any. Having met the parties prior to the opening, so to speak, the mediator has to make a decision whether to have an opening at all. It is not necessary in all cases to get all parties in one room together in order to have a formal opening. Many mediators simply separate the parties and speak to them each in turn.

If there are attorneys present, or other persons who have been through mediation before, the mediator can ask them whether they want to meet in joint session at the opening, or whether they would prefer to commence with a private session. Many times, the parties do not wish to meet each other in order to "vent" or for any other reason. One reason they have come to a mediator may be precisely because they do not wish to meet together but merely wish to get to a resolution of the problem so that they can part and go on their separate ways.

Another view is that the less the mediator says, the better. Yet the mediator should consider that the parties have not come to the mediation to listen to the mediator, they have come to be listened to, and it is usually unnecessary for the mediator to make more than a brief introduction. The same observation applies if attorneys are present; they prefer to talk rather than to listen. The sooner the mediator allows the attorneys and the parties to begin telling their story, the better they will like it.

The textbooks stress that the opening is an opportunity for the mediator to establish trust and credibility, but it may work just as well for the mediator to assume those qualities and, after the briefest of introductions, ask the participants to tell their story. Some mediators feel it necessary, if a party is represented by an attorney, nevertheless to ask the party directly to tell his story. However, this requires some sensitivity. The attorney is present in the room because his client is paying him to be there. The attorney has a job to do and may not particularly care for it if the mediator starts having a conversation directly with his client without clearing it with him first. Engaging both of them in conversation is more likely to be fruitful, but initially address one's remarks to the attorney, perhaps taking a moment to explain to the client that you as mediator want to proceed in a manner that both of them, attorney and client, feel will be most helpful to them.

That then empowers the attorney, if she so wishes, to invite her client to tell the story to the mediator. Or, if they prefer, the attorney will do the talking on behalf of her client. Or, as more often happens, they will share the task of communicating; usually, the attorney will approach it from the legal perspective, as she has been trained and is paid to do so, and her client will approach it from a more personal perspective. This is helpful to the mediator. It is much more helpful to the mediator to listen carefully to what is being said than to do much talking himself. The more they talk, the more they will provide clues to the mediator that will be very helpful in the final step of mediation, which is to achieve closure.

Whether the mediator has a joint opening session, to allow both parties to communicate across the table, depends upon the dynamics of the particular dispute. The mediator will bear in mind that there are fundamentally two kinds of disputes.

First is the dispute between strangers who have become entangled and need to be disentangled so that they can go their own ways.

Second is the dispute that is the product of an ongoing relationship; the mediator intervenes in the middle of something that may have a long history and necessarily has a different purpose with a different question: Can this dispute be creatively resolved so as to save or even enhance the relationship? Or, if the relationship must come to an end, can it be accomplished in such a way as to unburden the parties rather than leave them bitter and disappointed?

The mediator has to assess the situation and has very little time in which to do so, so she has to go with her instinct or gut feeling. The worst thing that can happen is that she will make a mistake; if she makes a mistake by having a joint opening session, and the parties yell at each other and make things worse, then it was just a mistake that needs to be recovered from during the next hour or so. Or if she makes a mistake by separating the parties, when they really wanted to talk to each other, perhaps they will speak up and tell her, in which case that mistake is easily corrected. The mediator need not be afraid of making a mistake, because she will have to make many decisions of this nature during the course of the mediation, and the more she steps up boldly to the function of making each decision, the better she will get at it. She just has to make a move.

"One thing I've learned in all my years; sometimes you just gotta say 'what the fuck', and make your move."

—says the 17-year old hero in
Risky Business, movie

It is possible to commence an opening session jointly with participants and have one participant use that occasion to attack the other party verbally in such a way as to greatly diminish the possibility of achieving resolution. It is desirable for a mediator to avoid that eventuality. There is no magic law that says it is always a good thing to permit a party to vent at the other party. People sometimes go to a therapist with a need to vent their rage against a parent who is deceased; the therapist does not say, "Sorry, there's no point in venting, because your father is not here to hear it." People do not have a constitutional right to yell at each other, unless they both decide they want to. The best way to make a person feel safe is to treat him with respect, to listen to him, and to acknowledge what he has to say.

It is not hard to show respect and empathy. The dispute into which the parties are unwillingly locked together is often not unlike the knot into which we have sometimes unwittingly tied ourselves; their self-inflicted wounds are not unlike the wounds we have sometimes inflicted on ourselves, and their predicament is the human condition expressed within the formal context of a dispute.

Sometimes people talk of war but dream of peace. They say they are willing to fight to the bitter end, but the expression itself is revealing: the end is often bitter. They want to put the matter behind them, but they don't know how. When a person "breaks out with a lamentable cry," we want to respond, "Take off the burden, lay it down," but we soon discover it is not so simple; such burdens are hard to shed. We have to be faithful to the process because the process is designed to overcome impasse after impasse, and the skill of the mediator is to master and apply the process.

Attorneys often assist parties during mediation. People have varying opinions of lawyers. Some writers have been quite scathing. Edward Gibbon wrote,

> It is dangerous to entrust the conduct of nations to men who have learned from their profession to consider reason as the instrument of dispute, and to interpret the laws according to the dictates of private interest, and the mischief has been felt even in countries where the practice of the law may be deserved to be considered as a liberal profession.

> —The History of the Decline and
> Fall of the Roman Empire

Oscar Wilde also had no fondness of lawyers or judges:

> A man whose desire is to be something separated from himself, to be a Member of Parliament or a successful grocer or a prominent solicitor or a judge, or something equally tedious, invariably succeeds in being what he wants to be. That is his punishment. Those who want a mask have to wear it.

> —De Profundis

RESPECTING THE ATTORNEY–CLIENT RELATIONSHIP

The mediator does well to respect the relationship between attorney and client and to recognize that attorneys have a challenging, usually stressful, and often essential job to perform. Everyone wants their own lawyer to be cunning, ferocious, and triumphant—yet really nice to them. If you visit Inner Temple Gardens in London, which has been the haunt of lawyers for hundreds of years, you will find in a quiet spot near the river an ancient statue of a naked little boy. He is reading a book and, if you peep over his shoulder, you can read the words at which he is forever staring: "Lawyers were children once." Countries without lawyers are generally countries without laws, ruled by tyrants. Proceedings without lawyers are often chaotic. The role of lawyers in dispute resolution is to make orderly an inherently confused situation and to help their clients achieve the best possible result in the circumstances. Just as the mediator needs to respect the human predicament of the disputants, she needs also to respect and work with the professional role of the attorney.

THE COST OF SETTLEMENT VIEWED AS AN INSURANCE PREMIUM

To achieve resolution, each side has to give up some of what is on its wish list. If you go to court, you are going to either win or lose. There are no compromises in front of a jury or in front of an arbitrator. There is a winner and a clear loser, and the winner may walk away very happy, but the loser is often in a very difficult position. A judgment in court can also be the subject of a costly and time-consuming appeal. To avoid these risks, people seek to settle their differences through mediation.

When you settle a dispute, each side in effect is paying a premium to the other side to avoid the risk of an unfavorable outcome at trial. The plaintiff takes less than might have been achieved at trial; the defendant pays more than would be achieved at trial if there was a defense verdict. Each side gives up a certain amount to avoid risk, and this is an important purpose of mediation.

COMMUNICATION

Where do you come from? asked the King.
From the subterranean passage where Gold is found, said the Snake.
What is more precious than Gold? asked the King.
Light, answered the Snake.
What is more refreshing than Light? asked the King.
Conversation, said the Snake.

—J. W. Goethe,
The Green Snake and the Beautiful Lily

fter the convening and the opening, the third stage of negotiation is called "communication," which is another way of saying "conversation."

If the negotiation is mediated, there are several possible methods of communication. One is that the parties communicate with each other in the presence of the mediator. The other is that each side communicates separately, privately, with the mediator. In addition, if one side consists of more than one person, then they may also wish to communicate privately between themselves.

Often, the pattern of communication during mediation includes all of them, joint, separate, and private, and usually the mediator is called upon to orchestrate the flow. The mediator's objective in all this is to establish momentum, enough momentum to carry the parties toward the next stage, which is negotiation. That is not to say that the parties do not engage in any negotiating during the communication stage, and communication takes place at every stage. These stages tend to overlap and are set forth for the sake of convenience. There is nothing carved in stone about the way mediation needs to be conducted, but this is a common analysis and works well in most instances.

There are two broad categories of communication.

The first is talking about the situation itself, the objective problem, and the history of events leading to the present impasse; often, legal issues and analyses are discussed. There is always some kind of impasse by the time the matter reaches mediation; parties do not need a mediator to help them with something they could easily accomplish themselves. Mediation starts with impasse and moves from one impasse to another, until by incremental stages the parties move closer toward resolution and finally achieve it. The skill of the mediator, applied to the process, with a view to helping the parties overcome the barriers to resolution, is how she adds value to the process. Working through the objective problem generally requires analytical skills.

The second category is not so much about the objective situation but about the parties' feelings, attitudes, emotions, and reactions toward what has happened to them. Parties very often express their situation in the passive tense: "This is what happened to me." Working through the subjective problem generally requires intuitive skills.

Sometimes the dispute started with an event fairly minor or even trivial but has escalated. A primary reason for escalation is the individuals' reactions to what happened, their emotions, feelings, and attitudes, so that by the time they reach mediation, they are suffering from a sense of injury or grievance, which overwhelms their ability to think rationally about how to resolve the situation. If attorneys or other advisors are involved in the mediation, it will be found that these professionals tend to concentrate more on the objective aspects, and the parties tend to concentrate more on their subjective feelings.

This is not always so. Sometimes the attorneys themselves have become riled up or irritated, often by the perceived behavior of opposing counsel. Attorneys vary a great deal in their relationship with their own clients, so sometimes they will give voice to their client's feelings of grievance and outrage, but more commonly they will attempt to promote a rational discussion. Having been trained in legal thinking during their years in law school, attorneys are bound by their training and by their professional responsibilities to analyze every conflict in terms of its legal significance and ramifications. Also, it should be acknowledged that there are many times when a party is prepared to view the conflict in mostly rational terms, seeking a resolution through dialogue, without feeling any great degree of emotional upset concerning it.

Nor is any judgment being made that a rational way of looking at a conflict is necessarily preferable to an emotional way of doing so. It is natural that human beings have subjective reactions to events in which they have been involved, and indeed one of the often mentioned failings of the legal system is that it seeks to banish human emotion, a litigant's feelings and attitudes, from the courtroom, leaving only the facts to be discussed together with the legal conclusions to be drawn. This desiccation of the manner in which conflicts are resolved in courts of law is one of the reasons for the growth in mediation.

The challenge for the mediator is how to allow, or help, all parties to say what they need to say without the mediation turning into therapy, that is to say, while maintaining at least a loose structure, but most important a momentum, a progression, toward a result. The mediator is under pressure as well. His situation is not like a psychotherapist's, whose patient may return week after week for an indeterminate period. It does not matter to the therapist how long the patient wishes to spend exploring his inner world, because it is understood that therapy may be a lengthy process; usually the result to be achieved in therapy is an increase in awareness, self-esteem, and confidence. But in mediation, the parties have come to it because they have some motivation to resolve a particular conflict, always involving another person, and because something worse is on their horizon if they do not resolve it.

It is often said that an important purpose of this stage of the mediation is to allow the parties to "vent," or express their frustrations and upsets in a safe environment; for sure, they will never be able to do this in court. Certainly, this is an important part of mediation, and if the mediator is practiced in the art of active listening, is prepared to give the party his entire attention, without interruption, without judgment, without agreement or disagreement and yet with empathy and acknowledgment, then a great deal of unburdening may be accomplished, sufficient at least to allow that party to weigh seriously the benefits of resolving the conflict once and for all.

The mediator needs to consider whether, in allowing one party to vent, it will serve any useful purpose for allowing that process to occur in the presence of the other party. Mediation may not seem a safe environment to a person who is obliged to sit and listen to his opposing party vent emotions, feelings, and attitudes. This is a matter that the mediator should be concerned about, not wishing to make things worse but wishing to make things better and wishing to facilitate the resolution of the conflict. Sometimes it is important that the parties do their venting in each other's presence so that each may hear how the other has been upset by the situation.

A great deal depends upon whether this is a relationship that will end once resolution is achieved or whether this is to be an ongoing relationship that has been disrupted by the particular conflict. If the latter, then it may be entirely necessary for the parties to vent face-to-face so that their inner subjective feelings may be exposed to each other, because often only in this way can healing and reconciliation be achieved. Where there is to be a continuing relationship, or the parties contemplate a continuing relationship, then it is important that there be more than just settlement—a reconciliation.

But when the parties do not intend any continuation of their relationship, and merely wish to have the dispute settled so that they can move their separate ways, then they generally do not have any interest in hearing about each other's emotional reactions to what has happened.

How does a mediator decide? She decides by asking the parties, because the mediator cannot be expected to guess or to know what to do without first inquiring as to the parties' preferences. Sometimes the mediator makes a mistake; sometimes the parties make a mistake. Sometimes they decline to speak when they should have. Sometimes they want to speak, but it only makes things worse. It is okay for mistakes to be made. The thing to do is to recover from the mistake and move on.

Some mediators feel that they need to ask a great many questions, in order themselves to find out all there is to know about the parties and the dispute. However, this somewhat misconceives what the mediator is there for. She is not there to become a complete expert in the subject matter of the dispute. She is there to help the parties resolve it, and the way to do this is not to act as an examiner, but to invite the parties to tell her whatever they wish.

When the parties have explained to the mediator what they need to say, when they have unburdened themselves to an extent that they deem sufficient, then it may be possible to go to the fourth stage of mediation, which is negotiation.

The art of the mediator is to listen actively to the parties, to let them know that they have been understood, and to keep the momentum of the mediation going so that the parties get to the stage where they recognize that they need to move from their positions, that they need to negotiate toward a satisfactory outcome.

LISTENING

Listening can be hard work. It is tempting to fake it. People try to avoid listening by talking themselves, or by fixing a "listening expression" on their faces and then thinking about something else. In a confrontational situation, when one person is talking, the other is often thinking what to say next. Some people find it so hard to listen that they never let the other person finish a sentence.

If a mediator were to choose to practice paying attention and listening with concentration and focus, this would be a foundation on which all else could be built. Without these skills, there is no genuine connection.

"If the person you are talking to doesn't appear to be listening, be patient. It may simply be that he has a small piece of fluff in his ear."

—Pooh Bear

TWENTY ONE

NEGOTIATION

I f war is the continuation of diplomacy by other means, then negotiation is war waged with kisses.

At last, the parties start negotiating in earnest, though they may not yet be in the Zone of Possible Agreement. The whole of the previous part of the negotiation has concentrated their minds on the problem; has filled them with the details of the conflict; and finally, with more or less help from the mediator, has convinced them that the reason they came to mediation in the first place—namely, to resolve their conflict—is worth achieving.

The previous stage may have taken five minutes, five hours or five months, but it must have led to a realization on the part of all concerned that, to achieve resolution of the conflict, or to achieve reconciliation in the case of a continuing relationship, they are going to have to change. They are going to have to move from their cherished positions. They are going to have to make concessions, because mediation is a voluntary, not a coercive, process. The price of settlement is that both sides have to agree, and for them to reach agreement, they both have to move. That is what negotiation is all about.

Negotiation is work. Negotiation means business, literally. The word derives from the Latin *neg* "not" and *otium* "leisure." It is not leisure. Dictionary definitions include (1) to deal or bargain with another or others; (2) to arrange for or bring about by discussion and settlement of terms; (3) to manage: transact: conduct; (4) to move through, around, or over in a satisfactory manner.

Negotiation theory tells us that there are, broadly, two types of bargaining: (1) distributive and (2) integrative. These words do not describe the process well, but they are commonly used in negotiation terminology.

Distributive bargaining takes place when there is a fixed amount or quantity to be divided between the parties. If a larger share is distributed to one party, then a smaller share is distributed to the other party. So any gain on the part of one side is met by a perceived loss on the other side. In a traffic accident case, whatever the defendant must pay is a loss to that defendant; the more the plaintiff is paid, the greater his perceived success. One side's gain is the other side's loss. This is called negotiating shares of a fixed "pie." It is competitive, not cooperative.

Integrative bargaining is conceived of in a different way. Here, the "pie" is not conceived as being a fixed quantity. Often, in business negotiations, for example, parties will brainstorm with each other, more cooperatively than competitively, in order to discover ways in which each can benefit more by the relationship than if they decide not to do business. Here, the endeavor is to explore underlying interests and needs, and discuss ways in which each side's needs and interests can be met cooperatively to the benefit of both.

This effort to "expand the pie" can sometimes be done in distributive bargaining as well. For example, it is not always just about the money. Sometimes a party wants something valuable to him, of no great concern to the other side. In a partnership breakup, one of them was extremely concerned that she keep the four cats that they had cared for together—after the other party was persuaded not to use this as a bargaining chip, but simply to make the concession graciously, she was then rewarded by the gratitude of the first one, who was then prepared to make a significant concession of her own. If parties can be persuaded to explore creative ways of satisfying each other's interests, in order to achieve resolution, they and the mediator will find this a most rewarding exercise.

CHESS PLAYERS, POKER PLAYERS, AND CHICKEN

People negotiate in different ways. Some analysts like to classify them into poker players versus chess players. A poker player hides his hand, seeks to bluff and deceive, and often is only willing to discuss dollar numbers and disdains discussing issues, concerns, or underlying interests. Chess players cannot conceal because all pieces are visible on the board. Chess is a game of strategic skill, and though chess players also engage in emotional gamesmanship, it is easy to see that there is a fundamental difference between a poker style and a chess style.

It may be difficult when a poker player runs into a chess player. The process of negotiation itself becomes more difficult because of those very different styles. The mediator has to mediate the different styles of negotiation to keep the process moving along. However, it is well to realize that these two descriptions, poker and chess, are just metaphors for what goes on in a conflict between human beings, whether expressed in the legal arena or not. A few people are neither chess nor poker players, but play the game of chicken. The actor James Dean played chicken in the movie Rebel Without A Cause; the driver who swerved last or not at all won the game. Chicken is a dangerous game. It is a deadly game of bluff, and not a good way to conduct negotiations.

Negotiators are on a continuum from very competitive to very cooperative. Studies show that aggressive negotiators may be effective or ineffective. Likewise, cooperative negotiators may be effective or ineffective. The particular style is not determinative. It seems that the best negotiators are capable of being competitive or cooperative as the occasion demands, often during the same negotiation.

REAL AND PERCEIVED WOUNDS

Although chess and poker are taken extremely seriously, they do not generally involve the kinds of injuries, losses, betrayals, wounds, and slights that are the common stuff of conflict. In real-life conflicts, we are dealing with real or perceived wounds, slights, insults, losses, injuries, and damages, and each such conflict has a history, which can be expressed in four ways:

1. One party's objective perception of what happened.

2. That same party's subjective reaction to what has happened.

3. The other party's objective perception of what happened.

4. That party's reaction to the event.

Sometimes people are quite unable to change their minds. That is why many people say, "Let the judge decide, let the jury decide, let an arbitrator decide." They cannot bear to let go of a position, and it is important to realize that when a person takes up a position—"I will take $100,000 and not a penny less"—that bald statement of position is fortified, supported, and buttressed by a whole array of intellectual arguments and emotional convictions.

The mediator will often find that, although parties may be present voluntarily—one of the three bedrock principles of mediation together with confidentiality and party control of outcome—that does not mean they will move willingly. A not-common expectation is that the other side will move and, therefore, although the mediator is not herself negotiating a resolution of the conflict, she needs to negotiate to some degree with each party, and with each attorney if one or more are present, to encourage, persuade, induce, or somehow get them to move closer to each other's positions.

AN ALLEGORY OF MOVEMENT

This process can be described allegorically as a valley surrounded by hills, with broken terrain, strewn with boulders and rocks, some trees and other vegetation, with a clearing in the middle set up as a boxing ring. At first the parties take up their positions on opposing hills and shoot at each other. Then they come down into the valley, and each takes up a secure position. One makes a dart toward a boulder that provides cover, whereas the other takes up a position behind a tree. Each position is given up unwillingly; each is fortified with emotional convictions and intellectual arguments. By a series of moves, large or small, the parties gradually approach the boxing ring in the middle of the valley. Finally they climb into the ring, which is where the real negotiation takes place and settlement occurs. The ring is the zone of possible agreement. To reach the ZOPA, they have already passed through several outer zones. With a Shakespearean or literary allusion for each zone, these are:

1. Unwillingness to move from a fixed position; expressions of righteousness and blame. "I am a man more sinned against than sinning." —*King Lear*

2. Talking to self, inward musing. "I am a very foolish, fond, old man." —*King Lear*

3. Consideration of what worse might befall. "I am in blood stepped in so far, That should I wade no more, Returning were as tedious as go o'er." —*Macbeth*

4. Recognition of commonality with others; for many people, this is a great leap forward. "I eat with bread, like you, feel want, taste grief, need friends." —*Richard II*

5. Offers exchanged that are "out in left field," "out of the ballpark," "in the wrong zip code," that are perceived not as credible but ridiculous, even insulting. This is a dangerous moment; the skill of the mediator at this point is to keep things moving. One party makes a move that the other side perceives as unreal, and therefore as not an offer at all. "And she said: Give me the head of John the Baptist." —Gospel of St. Mark 6:24-25

6. Offers that are within some range of credibility but not perceived as reasonable. Lady Capulet: "The valiant Paris seeks you for his wife. What say you, can you love the gentleman?" Juliet: "I'll look to like, if looking liking move." —*Romeo & Juliet* - Shakespeare

7. Offers perceived as not unreasonable, but not within the Zone of Possible Agreement. "Shylock, there's thrice thy money offered thee." —*The Merchant of Venice* - Shakespeare

8. ZOPA; once the parties have reached this stage, it is more than likely that they will achieve resolution of their conflicts. Bottom: "Let me play the lion too. I will roar that I will do any man's heart good to hear me." Quince: "You can play no part but Pyramus; for Pyramus is a sweet-faced man." Bottom: "Well, I will undertake it."—*A Midsummer Night's Dream* - Shakespeare

PARABLE OF THE ORANGE (SEARCH FOR UNDERLYING INTERESTS)

Teachers like to emphasize the difference between zero-sum negotiation and interest-based negotiation. A zero-sum negotiation is one in which each party's gain is at the expense of the other party. An interest-based negoti-ation is one in which there is room for compromise so that the respective interests of all the parties can be substantially satisfied.

Therefore, teachers tell mediators always to look for the underlying interests, so they tell the parable of the orange. The parable of the orange states that two sisters get into a fight over an orange, because each wants to use the orange in a recipe. There is only one orange. When the mediator arrives, she asks the elder sister what she needs the orange for, and that sister replies that she needs the juice in order to bake a certain recipe. Then the mediator asks the younger sister what she needs the orange for and gets the reply that she needs the orange peel in her recipe. So the brilliant mediator says to the sisters, "You can each have what you need, you can each satisfy your respective interests, all we need to do is juice the orange for the elder sister's recipe, and the peel will be left over to be used in the younger sister's recipe."

This is a very exciting prospect and, if it were possible to settle all dis-putes in this manner, we would live in a better, happier world. However, in the real world, it is exceedingly seldom that the orange can be divided so neatly into the juice and the peel to satisfy completely the interests of the disputing sisters.

The real-world problem is hardly ever so tidy. In the parable, the sisters' needs do not overlap at all. Both of them can be completely satisfied, with the added advantage that, if one of them took the entire orange, part of it would go to waste, whereas in the parable the entire orange is used to best effect. Also, in real-world disputes there is often an underlying tension between the parties that has nothing to do with the orange itself. Such problems do not readily yield to simple problem-solving technique. For example, the elder sister might resent the younger for unstated reasons; she might not want to make any deal that works for her sister. The younger sister may know that the elder sister never cooks at all and is only pretending to want to use part of the orange in order to frustrate the younger sister. The dispute over the orange may have nothing to do with the real difficulties between the two.

In practice, it will be found that some negotiations are single issue and that it is not possible to get to the underlying interests because there are not any. Also, where parties have a dispute to resolve before they can go on their separate ways, they are generally more interested in zero-sum bargaining. But where the relationship between the parties must necessarily continue into the future, or where the preservation of the relationship is an important factor in the negotiation, it will be found that multiple interests may be brought into play in order to fashion solutions broadly satisfactory to everyone.

Before people can even embark on a problem-solving mode, they need to spend time on two other factors: (1) how to position themselves in the negotiation so that they are taken seriously, and (2) how to get the other side into a position of being willing to cooperate in a problem-solving endeavor.

Five assumptions are often expressed in the ideal world and are not necessarily found at all in the real world: (1) focus on the problem, (2) figure out what you really want, (3) be willing to engage in a mutual trade-off negotiation, (4) people will operate out of enlightened self-interest, and (5) creative ideas carry the day.

It is not always possible to focus on the problem until a very considerable way into the negotiation. Parties come to negotiations with unspoken wants and expectations. Negotiators have established ways of doing things, which may conflict. People have certain standards of conduct that are unarticulated even by them. There are power differences between parties, which make it difficult for the parties to be honest and forthright with each other.

Parties are not always clear about what they want. Their goals may change during the course of the negotiation, as different facets come to light. When people focus on a particular situation intensely over a period of time, their attitudes can undergo considerable change, and although this is part of the goal of the mediator, it also means that their desires and wants may change as well. The parties may not always grasp the scope and implications of the situation that they are in.

Willingness to negotiate is a great thing, but it can itself be a problem unless both parties arrive at the point of being willing to negotiate at the same moment. If one party is willing to negotiate but the other is not, not only does the first party feel at a disadvantage but her overtures may be rejected.

Parties may, and usually do, act out of their own perceived self-interest, but the phrase "enlightened self-interest" is highly ambiguous. What is meant by enlightenment, in the context of the negotiation? Creative ideas would carry the day if rationality prevailed at the bargaining table, but it does not always do so. Feelings, attitudes, and emotions intrude, as well as remembered slights and personal preoccupations.

There are all kinds of hidden needs, wants, preoccupations, concerns, and the assorted baggage that is generally hidden from view, not only to the mediator but also to the other party, and even to the party herself, that get in the way of the process of getting to "yes."

The mediator having developed her existing faculty of emotional intelligence soon comes to recognize that something else is going on; this is the subject of shadow negotiation.

SHADOW NEGOTIATION

A shadow is something that follows you around. It is everything that isn't being said. It is what is really going on, getting in the way of what should be going on. Whatever is not on the table is under the table. Most people in most negotiations spend most of the time groping under the table, trying to come to grips with it. It is the shadow. It has to be dealt with. Lots of people make lots of money explaining to other people how to deal with the shadow; usually they get it wrong. Carl Jung spent much of his career writing about it. In essence, the negotiation is mostly with oneself.

> *Each of us has an original, you see, living somewhere underneath the shadow of our daily life. That life we live in the moving world is the dream life of the copy.*
>
> —Louise Erdrich,
> *Four Souls*

This baggage train that is carried by nearly everyone into every negotiation constitutes a shadow negotiation, that continues side by side and simultaneously with the "real negotiation" and is generally more important. Often the real negotiation cannot resolve until at least parts of the shadow negotiation have been resolved. The parties in a negotiation are in a relationship with each other, if only by virtue of the negotiation itself, and often by virtue of what has previously happened between them, and all these "shadows" are being negotiated at the same time as they try to solve what is perceived to be the difficulty between them.

Parties second-guess themselves; they are overly optimistic or unduly pessimistic. They may sell themselves short. They may be unduly belligerent. They may be too talkative or not talkative enough. They may constantly get in their own way. There may be power imbalances that are almost impossible to negotiate, in the sense of ensuring a level playing field.

All these things must be taken into account when dealing with a real-world negotiation. If it were not this way, there would be no need for mediators. The reason to have a mediator in the first place is not to come up with a bright, brilliant idea that solves the problem and ties it up neatly in a ribbon. The reason that the mediator is there, with all her expertise and skills, is to observe and recognize the multiple dynamics going on even in the simplest mediation and do what is necessary to make it possible for the parties to achieve resolution.

FAILURE OF PROBLEM-SOLVING STRATEGIES

Problem-solving strategies have an important place and yet may fail for a number of reasons, mainly because, although the subjective always gets annoyingly in the way of the objective solution, in human relationships subjective reality is what counts. The rest, if not exactly illusion, is not exactly reality either and is nowhere near as important as human connection. Watch out for these problem areas:

- Lack of attention to context.

- Lack of attention to interrelationships.

- Failure to anticipate side effects.

- Failure to anticipate long-term repercussions of decisions.

- Thinking in terms of isolated cause-and-effect relationships.

- The cumulative effects of numerous small judgmental mistakes.

- Overgeneralizations.

- Low tolerance for uncertainty.

- Ignoring emotions.

- Solving the problem we can solve instead of the one we ought to solve.

- Ignoring or explaining away contrary evidence.

RHETORIC

The three elements of rhetoric—set forth by the Greek philosopher Aristotle in the 4th century B.C.—are logos, pathos and ethos. These three words have acquired various interpretations over the centuries, but the basic distinction is mind, body, and spirit. The successful integration of these three qualities makes for successful rhetoric, which makes for successful persuasion.

LOGOS

Logos has a long history going back to the millennium before Christ. It has acquired a number of different but related meanings. Logos refers to the mind, and to logic and reason, regarded as the products of the mind. Logos was the subject of inquiry of many classical Greek philosophers, and also by later Christian writers, and has been subject to many differing interpretations, including "word," as set forth in the Gospel of St. John: "In the beginning was the word, and the word was with God, and the word was God." For the purposes of negotiation, Logos is the essential tool of reason that leads to effective persuasion and thus effective results. Logos in the absence of pathos or ethos tends towards pedantry and corporate-speak and bureaucracy. Logos unmediated by pathos or ethos gives reason a bad name.

PATHOS

Logos without pathos is pedantry, but pathos without logos is demagoguery.

Pathos is the expression of emotion that can bring strong men to tears and set great events in motion though not necessarily in the right direction. Pathos appeals to the gut. Some say that pathos lives in the heart, while others insist that logos resides there, but neither is correct for the heart encompasses all. Poorly done, which is often, Pathos degenerates into sentimentality. It can be overblown. It can be insincere. It can be faked, and depending on the audience it may be effective or it may do more harm than good. But genuine pathos is powerful indeed. Pathos unconnected to logos is anarchic, apt to be destructive, and can easily get out of control. That is why many books on emotion treat it as a kind of disorder that requires careful handling. One book advises that in the presence of emotion one should take a deep breath, count to ten, and call for a break in the proceedings. This kind of advice is written from the perspective of fear, namely fear of emotion itself. President Franklin Roosevelt touched on this in 1933 when he said: "The only thing we have to fear is fear itself."

Pathos by itself is untethered, unmoored. It is anarchic in the literal sense of that word—leaderless. Some people are emotional in that chaotic way, which only means that logos is not involved, and probably ethos is not either. That does not mean that one needs to take a deep breath, count to ten, and then take a walk outside. It means only that the Logos of the mediator is needed to supply the necessary integration in order to make pathos serve the interests of the whole person. Nor does this mean that it is necessary for logos to control pathos. The excessive control of logos is the reason that whole societies allow their emotional lives to become stunted and suppressed. Much of the difficulty arising from interpersonal relationships is not that there is too much emotion, but too little expression of it. Pathos needs a restraining influence and finds it in logos, the Word. Logos is the mind's product. It is a thinking machine. It may think rationally or irrationally. It may think in an untrained fashion. There can be many things wrong with logos. It can think with too much information or too little. Both logos and pathos need to consider the demands of the heart. It is true that pathos cannot think, but it is also true that logos cannot feel. Thinking without feeling can be deadly. Feeling without thinking is a prescription for chaos. There is no substitute for developing a relationship between logos and pathos that will serve the interest of the whole person.

ETHOS

Ethos means "presence," and ethos completes the triumvirate of rhetoric that can go forth and conquer. Just as pathos has its strengths but also liabilities, so also the abilities of logos come at a price. Logos has no real sense of what is right and what is wrong. It lacks that fine sense of balance and judgment that makes right action possible. Ethos is the directing hand or animating presence. Ethos is the observer and the place where distinctions and judgments can be made. Ethos lives with aesthetics and derives from the Greek word for observer. Ethos is the essential ingredient of authenticity. Ethos is the one who observes, but also the one ultimately in the position to influence the outcome of events. Ethos is able to integrate the forces of logos and pathos, and ultimately is able to direct whether those forces are to be used for proper ends. Applying this to rhetoric and the attempt to persuade others to a point of view or course of action, one sees that a passionate, emotional argument without direction cannot achieve its result, and likewise a dry, desiccated argument often also fails to convince. Reason and passion must be integrated and directed toward purpose; purpose is provided by ethos. Ethos supplies integrity. Integrity gives a person presence, and presence is a function of integrity.

Presence is not a matter of being tall or short, man or woman, of any particular race, color, or creed; it does not even have much, if anything, to do with education. It does not care if you are good looking or well dressed, rich or poor, high or low. It does not care because all these are external qualities, and integration is an internal matter of uniting heart, mind, and spirit toward the same object. Then one's rhetoric may be plain and simple or high-flown and flowery. It may be more emotional than rational or more intellectual than passionate; all those things are simply personal qualities of the particular utterance, but the distinguishing quality is the argument that comes from an integrated person who is able to direct the whole of her argument to the purpose at hand.

It is possible to fake emotion, and one has only to listen to a number of speakers to know that it is not hard to obfuscate rather than clarify. Sometimes a successful argument is not that rational; sometimes a rational argument does not have much emotional force behind it, but the most successful arguments combine logos and pathos, whereas Ethos supplies the purpose that lends the whole argument coherence. Even so, a sociopath may deliver brilliant speeches with rational argument supported by strong emotion, and some have great presence. So something else must be missing.

There must be some other quality, connecting ethos, logos, and pathos, that distinguishes great orators from the artifice of bad people who have simply mastered a skill. One might say that in the center of the triangle of rhetoric, we might find tucked away a potential hidden ingredient—Eros, the beating heart—that determines how great talents will be used. There are brilliant, heartless people who can get results, but to produce miracles, "Love Is All You Need" was one of the Beatles' great creations, and countless others have sung of love longed for, dreamed about, labored over, found, lost, and mourned.

> *Love is that liquour sweet and most divine, Which my God feels as blood; but I, as wine.*
>
> (George Herbert, 1633)

CLOSURE

"A man has got to know his limitations."

—movie, *Magnum Force*

S ettlement is a peace treaty declared on agreed terms. It represents the triumph of reality over illusion, rationality over expectation, calculation over emotion, and the cessation of conflict between parties who, in many cases, will go their separate ways.

Reconciliation is different from a peace treaty, and harder to achieve. It represents a collaborative harmonization of emotional needs and perceived realities, when the parties want or need to continue living in relationship with each other. In 1945, Europe—for millennia the cockpit of war—was devastated. Yet today most European nations with different languages, histories, and economies have achieved gradual reconciliation so thorough that today a general European war is hardly conceivable. Neither today can we conceive of Georgia attacking New Jersey or Alabama marching on Ohio. Permanent reconciliation is possible.

Without war we would have no word for peace, without peace no word for war. The classical Greek word for the natural state of things was *stasis*, from which we derive the word *static*, but to them meant perpetual conflict.

"People, I just want to say, you know, can we all get along? Can we stop making it horrible for the older people and the kids? I mean, we're all stuck here for a while. Let's try to work it out."

—spoken by Rodney King,
construction worker, during the
Los Angeles riots in 1992.

The mediator has the task of maintaining the process between the parties, whether the goal is settlement or reconciliation, through convening, opening, communicating, negotiating, until the final step, which is closure. And whatever may have been written about aesthetic elegance, it is also a fact that the mediator may have to effect closure with her bare hands, so to speak. It will be found that parties often negotiate to a short distance from each other, but the final step that each side has to make proves elusive. They are like horses that gallop right up to a jump but then screech to a halt, sometimes throwing the rider—and as far as mediation is concerned, this is a moment when the whole process may blow up.

At this final stage, suddenly emotion may again take over, and the impulses of the ego thrust themselves forward. With only a small concession needed to achieve resolution, the desire to win, to score a victory over the opponent, to stick it to the other side, to achieve a tiny measure of revenge, reasserts itself.

How is a mediator to proceed? Some mediators talk about the dignity of being able to say "No" and walk away. Others take the view that the dignity of saying No is an insufficient reward to exchange for the benefits of getting to Yes. Such mediators see, in their mind's eye, the parties as having entered the room with a great burden upon their backs, or a ball and chain around their ankle that, with just a little more effort, can be removed. Even if the parties, having settled, walk out of the room with some reluctance, which is called buyer's remorse or seller's remorse, the buyer wondering if she took too little, the seller wondering if she paid too much, the match is over. The reason the parties chose mediation in the first place was to achieve that cessation. It is not just a matter of money, and certainly not a matter of ego. There is a great deal of time and stress, and waste of energy and resources, involved in disputes, so the benefit the parties receive in the form of "getting their lives back" is huge.

TWENTY THREE

EXPERTISE AND THE POWER TO SEE THE INVISIBLE

Negotiation is a multiple decision-making process. Negotiation always occurs in the context of other people. It involves recognition that other people exist and have separate interests. Such recognition is generally absent in two-year-old toddlers, which is why they are called the Terrible Twos, because at that age the child goes through—one hopes—a short period of intense recognition of its own interests and utter inability to countenance the interests of others. Two-year-olds do not negotiate: they make inflexible demands and throw tantrums. Fortunately, this is a stage of development that soon passes, and parents who long to throttle their two-year-old are pleasantly enchanted with the three- and four-year-olds.

Some adults behave like two-year-olds. If they are also incessant liars, we identify them as sociopaths. It is difficult to negotiate with a two-year-old, and even harder to negotiate with a sociopath because of the additional factor of deception.

It is difficult to negotiate with a dictator because of the tendency to wind up dead. Hitler never entered into genuine negotiation; when he purported to do so, it was all a sham. For some people, entering into negotiation is never more than a ruse. Chamberlain thought he could negotiate with Hitler and returned waving a piece of paper that he called "peace in our time"; the paper was worthless. Chamberlain had failed to recognize the nature of the man he was dealing with. With untrustworthy negotiating partners, it is essential to reduce all agreements to writing enforceable by the court, but the better course is to avoid such people.

In any negotiation, the participants must be able to make the decisions that will move them in the direction of a mutually satisfactory outcome. Whether they like it or not, they need to take the other participants' interests into account in order to craft an agreement that everyone will sign.

The power to see the invisible is what we generally call *expertise*. Experts can see things invisible to the ordinary person. Patients rely upon their physician's power to tell them what is wrong with them, just as clients rely on their attorneys to help them through the legal labyrinth. Experts can notice patterns, anomalies, the big picture, opportunities, differences that are too small for novices to detect, and their own limitations.

The expert is aided in the task of recognizing significant patterns because of a knowledge base, built by both study and experience, that permits the expert to fit a series of seemingly unrelated facts into a coherent pattern, usually based on the template recognized as standard in that particular area of expertise. Pattern recognition is the ability to impose order upon a situation. When a patient goes to the doctor with a series of symptoms that are inexplicable yet frightening, the physician is able to take the chaos out of the situation by imposing a diagnosis. The diagnosis, even in the absence of any treatment, is comforting to a patient because it removes the discomfort of chaos. Lawyers perform the same function for their clients, building contractors for their customers, and so on.

An anomaly is something that should be there but isn't, or something that should not be there but is. An anomaly is something that needs explanation. In detective stories, anomalies are usually called clues. A famous literary example is Sherlock Holmes: "Did you hear that hound bark in the night, Watson?" "No, Holmes, I did not." "Precisely, my dear Watson." Since the dog always barked at strangers, the absence of barking was the clue Holmes needed to establish that the murderer was not a stranger.

In reading legal briefs, it is remarkable how easy it is for a skeptical mediator to notice what the brief writer is trying to conceal. In fact, noticing what is missing in a party's presentation of a case is almost an art form, which can be acquired by experience. It is such a natural tendency to omit or deemphasize weak points in one's own case that an experienced mediator would always look for those omissions, which are leverage points to move parties toward each other, because everyone has weaknesses in their own position—otherwise they would not bother to negotiate.

Similar to the power to notice patterns is the ability to have a sense of the big picture, which is also called *situation awareness*. We have colloquial expressions for this—"It is easy to lose sight of the big picture" and "It is hard to see the wood for the trees."

When parties come to a negotiation, they are quite often lost in the wood. There are so many trees, and they have gained such familiarity with each tree so that necessarily they know infinitely more than the mediator could ever know. The mediator lacks the advantage of knowing the trees, so he must bring another skill set to the table—being able to see the big picture and, in this way, help the parties find their way out of the dark wood.

We can readily see that there are therefore innumerable kinds of expertise, but in this society at this time extra knowledge is becoming fractured into smaller and smaller fragments, and there is a pressing need for the expert to see the big picture and to coordinate all of the elements within it in order to arrive at sound decisions.

Anyone can stand a mile away from a wood and say what it is, but that in itself does not amount to expertise. The true expert must also understand the way things work, and have the ability to see inside events and objects. It is not possible to become an expert merely by looking in from the outside. It is necessary to have been inside the big picture or many big pictures many times over a long period so that the expert can build up a mental model of what is going on inside, how it is actually working, the way it is supposed to work. That is why it is often said that a mediator needs to have some expertise in the area in which the dispute is being negotiated.

However, that level of expertise need not be as profound as the expertise of the parties to the negotiation, because a good mediator brings a different set of skills, and in that sense the ability to see the big picture, to spot anomalies and patterns, is more important than the need for as much expertise as the parties to the negotiation. Indeed, it can serve as an impairment or detriment, because the reason the parties are in the negotiation in the first place is that they need someone with a different perspective but who nonetheless has a good understanding of the language of the particular problem and an ability to understand the details, without necessarily knowing them all. Otherwise, it would be necessary for the mediator to track the entire dispute from day one until it arrives in the negotiating session, which of course is impossible. It is also unnecessary.

Finally, expertise requires the ability to recognize one's own limitations, which may also be called humility. No one knows everything. Even as to events that occurred in the past, we see that the ability to construct an exact picture of what happened is fraught with uncertainty. How much more uncertain is the future, and yet it is necessary whether we like it or not to move forward into the future, making the best decisions we can in the present based on the available information.

Yet the phrase "based on available information" is itself a potential trap. Some people use the absence of all conceivable information as an excuse for taking no action at all. Some people use the data-gathering process as a means of prolonging decision-making indefinitely. It is always possible to gather more data. The quantity of data is usually infinite if one looks hard enough. The amount of data that we need is that amount that permits us to take a decision resulting in action with some confidence that the action will produce the desired results, always with a caveat that we will watch the situation as it moves into the future and be ready to modify past decision by future action in order to cope with changing circumstances. This is the province of the true expert.

TWENTY FOUR

ILLUSIONS AND BLINDFOLDS

People are negotiating constantly to satisfactory conclusions, but people who come into mediation nearly always do so because they are at an impasse. Not only are they at an impasse, but they are also entangled with each other. After all, countless negotiations end satisfactorily with the parties doing business with each other and countless others do not, but the kind of impasse that ends in mediation is a conflict that the parties cannot simply walk away from.

A person may go into a car dealership to buy a car, but if the price or other terms are not right, she may walk away and go elsewhere; there was no entanglement. A dispute requiring mediation therefore contains two qualities: impasse and entanglement. Example: the Israelis cannot walk away from the Palestinians, and vice versa. One could say that impasse + entanglement = likelihood of violence.

There is something particular about people who are both entangled and at an impasse that makes them come to a mediator for help in achieving resolution. Certain factors distinguish these kinds of conflicts. First, one party cannot simply vanquish or overwhelm the other; each party has at least enough power to remain in the struggle. Second, neither party is willing simply to give in to the other, thus ending the conflict. Third, neither party can simply avoid or walk away from the conflict, or each has made the decision not to do so.

Another particular feature of such conflicts is that one or both of them is not seeing the situation clearly. One or both of them is wearing blindfolds or blinders, which are preventing them from clearly seeing the situation in which they are entangled.

Some people will always fight to maintain the status quo. They will fight for things not to change. They will fight for the good old days, the way we were, the comfortable, tried, and proven way of doing things. Sometimes they are called conservatives. In a litigated case, the defense would always prefer the status quo in preference to any other outcome; in other words, the defense would prefer the plaintiff simply to dismiss the suit. This is the *status quo blindfold*.

Sunk costs are a blindfold. When a person loses money on the stock market, the money is lost, sunk, gone. In a litigated case, when both sides have spent a great deal of money getting to the point that they have reached, these are sunk costs that are usually not recoverable. The fact that they have already spent these costs is a source of great vexation to many people and blindfolds them to the realities of their situation. On November 11, 1918, the Germans agreed to an Armistice with the Allies on extremely unfavorable terms. The enormous loss of life and the awful privations they had suffered during the war were sunk costs for the German people that caused them enormous bitterness in the years to come and in part led to a second war in which they hoped to recover those sunk costs. This is the *sunk cost blindfold*.

A third blindfold is the anchor. People are often anchored to their first impressions or to the first number they have put on the table. Plaintiffs make a demand and feel anchored to that demand, unwilling to move from it, and if they are forced to move a long way, they look back with some bitterness on the distance they have been forced to move. Likewise, defendants are apt to make a very low offer and then feel anchored to it, unwilling to move further. This is the *anchoring blindfold*. A clever negotiator can use anchoring to good effect, as long as she is willing for the first demand or offer to be perceived as reasonable, within the right ballpark or zip code. If the other party perceives that demand or offer as reasonable, even if not acceptable, it will tend to act as an anchor for the remainder of the negotiation.

Pride is a blindfold and has the particular quality in some people that anything said by the other side is used by pride to confirm itself. If one side says the sky is blue, this blindfold says yes, it is, and that helps me. If the other side says no, the sky is green, this anchor says certainly, and that also helps me. Whatever is said in order to introduce an element of reality to the situation is used by pride to confirm its own position or importance. This is the confirming evidence, or *pride blindfold*.

Anger is a blindfold that leads to an overly optimistic assessment of one's position. This is the overoptimistic, or *anger blindfold*.

Fear is a blindfold that leads to an unduly pessimistic evaluation of one's position. This is the over pessimistic, or *fear blindfold*.

Apathy or disgust are blindfolds, leading to an impulse to "give away the store" or "throw out the baby with the bathwater." This is the *apathy blindfold*.

People become wedded to a blindfold by the manner in which they frame the problem. This leads them to an improper assessment of the risk inherit in the situation. This could be called the *framing blindfold*.

All of these blindfolds affect the way people perceive the nature of the situational conflict they are involved in, which is one of the reasons why they have reached impasse and come to a mediator. Part of the mediator's job is to help them remove the blindfold so that they can see more clearly.

TWENTY FIVE

DECEPTION, DOUBT, AND CERTAINTY

"The world is not a solid continent of facts sprinkled by a few lakes of uncertainties, but a vast ocean of uncertainties speckled by a few islands of calibrated and stabilized forms"

—Reassembling the Social,
Bruno Latour 2005

Every negotiation oscillates between doubt and certainty. Parties seek certainty even though very often they are besieged by doubts. People entering negotiations experience apprehension, which is another word for fear, though fear expressed at a low level of intensity. The reason they have come to a mediator is because they did not feel able to achieve a negotiated result on their own. Therefore, a mediated negotiation is already, almost by definition, a negotiation either that has gone wrong or never begun or that has a doubtful prognosis.

During the course of most people's lives, they are negotiating at various times for various things, and millions of negotiations are accomplished every day without the need for the intervention of an experienced mediator. Thus from the outset we see that a mediated negotiation contains elements of difficulty that have led the parties to be willing to spend money on the expert services of a professional in the particular field.

Generally speaking, a party must experience doubt to arrive at a mediated solution. The experience of doubt is uncomfortable. The experience of certainty is much more pleasant. People seek certainty to avoid the pain of doubt. A party to a negotiation has usually achieved a measure of certainty with regard to the position that they are taking, and that certainty which is a mental state is fortified and buttressed by all kinds of considerations, feelings, emotions, attitudes, and arguments, all of which are themselves mental states.

However, the nature of a negotiation is that a mutually satisfied outcome can never be reached unless each party is prepared to change position. Such change involves movement from a well-fortified position into a position of doubt.

The process of moving from one position to another is mentally taxing, which is why the presence of a mediator can be of great help and comfort. As soon as the parties have arrived at a different position, they will dig in with all kinds of arguments and considerations, emotional ideas and attitudes, and they will gradually or rapidly achieve a degree of certainty about the new position that they have now assumed.

It may be necessary for the parties to move position many times before they reach the Zone of Possible Agreement. That is why they must oscillate between certainty and doubt again and again, and that is why many people would rather resort to conflict, precisely because it is possible to enter a conflict without ever having to change one's mind or experience the kind of mental tension that is involved in changing one's mind.

Many organizations, including government departments where the procedures for taking decisions are institutionalized and cumbersome, find it easier to leave the decision up to somebody else rather than go through the stress and trouble of taking decisions internally.

Many cases go to trial because one or the other or both of the parties are simply unwilling to engage in the difficult task of negotiating a settlement. The task of the mediator, if such parties are willing to enter into mediated negotiation, is to help them overcome the internal barriers to achieving the changes necessary to avoid a third-party outcome.

Of course, many times the reason a matter proceeds to trial or other conflict is because one or both of the parties have simply misread the situation in reality.

All negotiations have an internal and an external aspect. The internal aspect is the individual's own subjective reactions to what is going on. The external reality is what the legal system is designed to deal with; in fact, the legal system is designed to squeeze out of the process all mental or emotional reaction and to delineate only the facts that can be adduced in evidence that are relevant, that is to say, that have a bearing on the legal issue presented to the court. But here as well, the mediator has a vital role to play, in being a sounding board against which the parties can test the reality of their own view of the situation.

Thus, we see that parties may have a distorted view of reality, in addition to having inappropriate emotional attitudes to the problem. This is called the difference between the real negotiation and the shadow negotiation, and the expert mediator needs to be expert in dealing with these different aspects.

In this way, the task of the mediator is more complex than the task of a court, which has had all the emotional side of it squeezed out by the rules of evidence so that a dry problem can then be presented for a legal resolution. But such resolutions are often unsatisfactory to both sides, and they are always unsatisfactory to the losing side.

Although mediated negotiation is difficult, and often far more trying on the parties than a trial itself, it nonetheless has the exquisite advantage that it results in a solution arrived at by the parties themselves. Such negotiated resolutions are far more stable. They result not only in finality but also in a release of emotional burden on both sides. They are thus a healing experience and, to this extent, are a far more civilized and sophisticated method of resolving disputes than the legal system, which merely declares a winner and a loser.

THE USE AND ABUSE OF DECEPTION

The word *deceive* is derived from Latin, *de-* "away" + *capere* "to take," *decipere* "to ensnare, catch in a trap."

Deception is common in human relationships. Deception is common in negotiation. Most human relationships are conducted by way of negotiation.

"Women know how to fake orgasm. Men know how to fake an entire relationship."

—attributed to actress Sharon Stone

The most common form of deception is self-deception. The buyer deceives herself as to the value of what is to be bought, generally undervaluing it. The seller deceives herself as to the value of what is to be sold, generally overvaluing it.

Sellers use all kinds of techniques to convince a potential buyer that the object is worth the seller's valuation. Similarly, buyers use techniques to persuade the buyer to sell.

In a litigated case, the buyer is the defendant and the seller is the plaintiff. In effect, the plaintiff is selling the injury back to the defendant for a particular cost, which legally is called damages. The peculiarity of this situation is that the defendant buyer cannot walk away from the transaction. The defendant must either buy a settlement or face the risk of being forced to pay a valuation put on the injury by a court. The plaintiff seller also faces the same dilemma. There is only one potential buyer for the plaintiff's injury. If that buyer refuses to buy at the valuation put upon the injury by the plaintiff seller, then the plaintiff will be compelled to accept whatever valuation is put on the injury by the court.

Thus, the peculiarity of any litigated case is that neither party can walk away. There is only one potential buyer who is the defendant, and if the seller plaintiff chooses to walk away, then she will receive nothing. But the risk of loss is high. The national average is fifty-fifty.

Plaintiffs and defendants therefore use all means at their disposal, including self-deception, to persuade themselves that they will beat the national average. And it is certain that one of them is going to be correct. The uncertainty of litigated outcomes is the driving force behind the effort of parties to negotiate a satisfactory result between each other. It is an exercise in avoidance of risk.

There is also the matter of the expensive trial, because the costs associated are usually substantial and, whichever side wins in the end, both sides have lost a great deal in terms of financial costs, time expended, and the stress of going through with it, all of which add up to a powerful incentive to get the matter settled. And indeed, settlement rates are extremely high; less than five percent of litigated cases ever go to trial.

By no means do all negotiations relate to events that have already occurred. Indeed, most negotiations concern future events, but these are not the kinds of negotiation that usually require the assistance of a mediator. Most business people are entirely capable of mediating by themselves, and such negotiations are usually called *contract negotiations*, occurring many millions of times every year to work out amicable ways of profitable cooperation.

It is generally when things have gone wrong that the presence of a mediator is helpful; the reason for this is that when something is turned into a TGW (Thing Gone Wrong), there is always associated with it the upset, the emotional reaction of the parties to the difficulty.

People never enter into negotiation or dispute resolution with respect to matters in the past that have gone right. In mediation or in any situation in which one or more people are interacting, a person who pays attention will more easily detect truth from falsehood.

Even where people are not trying to deceive, and most people most of the time are not trying to deceive, the whole truth of what they are seeking to convey may not be apparent even to them, but to the listener who is paying attention the shadow truths are apparent more to the listener than to the speaker. Often, the speaker is working hard to convey her meaning but is not entirely sure what she wishes to communicate. The listener will pick up everything in the tail end of a sentence, a word here or there, an inflexion, a gesture, a throwaway line.

If the mediator is sitting there thinking of what she is going to say or do next, then she is paying attention to her own thought processes and not to what is being communicated.

Paying attention, if one is not absorbed in one's own problems is not terribly hard work but, on the contrary, has a light and airy quality. For example, a person enjoying a book or a movie or a piece of music or a football game is paying close attention but without a great deal of effort. It is easy to pay attention when one is interested in the subject matter.

The opposite of attention is distraction.

People's stories are not always consistent. That does not necessarily mean they are lying. It means their own perception of events alters as they focus their own attention on such events, bearing in mind that such events nearly always happen in the past and are preserved in memory. Because consistency is so valued in our society, when parties engage in the game of winning and losing, which they do at trial because trial always results in a winner or a loser, the attempt is always to catch the opponent in an inconsistency.

But catching people out in inconsistencies is not the mediator's game at all. She knows that when a person concentrates her mind on a past event, the perception of that event will change over time. Different aspects will be brought into memory, even over the course of a single day; varying interpretations of what happened may emerge. Also, people express something a particular way and an hour later will talk about the same thing in a slightly different way. The complete mediator takes this all in without harsh judgment.

People who lie all the time are sociopaths, also called psychopaths. They are not very common. Because they do it all the time, they are extremely good at lying. Their whole life is based on the ability to deceive people. Therefore, sociopaths may present themselves very well and sound convincing. But as they proceed, because they do not tell the truth, the story does not add up. A detail here, a detail there, a huge inconsistency that is then sought to be explained, building up over time, will teach any mediator unfortunate enough to run into such a person that she is dealing with someone quite dangerous. Behind the ordered façade and smiling face of a psychopath lie chaos and evil intentions. Such a person will not settle a case. Such a person will probably not attend mediation.

Everyone gets subjective perceptions mixed up with objective reality from time to time. The difference lies in the extremity of the psychopath. It should not be assumed that people who are inconsistent or confused or who do not tell the truth are necessarily psychopaths. Most people most of the time are quite ordinary. Nearly everyone is in the ordinary range. At one end of the range are psychopaths and criminals, at the other geniuses and saints. Most of us are in the middle, and mediators will have to deal with what is normal nearly all the time.

If a mediator finds herself falling into doubt and confusion, which cannot be sorted out by the exercise of reason, persuasion, further study and attempts to bring order into the situation, then she may have reason to suspect what is going on.

Doubt is not necessarily a bad thing. Doubt has a bad rap because it is uncomfortable. It is the fork in the road, without clear directions which way to proceed. But doubt is the mediator's friend, as it is the friend of all explorers in any field. Doubt itself has a friend, which is hope.

Without hope, doubt can result in paralysis, a complete inability to move at all. Certainty also generally results in no movement, because why should one move if one is certain of where one is. Christopher Columbus had hope, so he moved even though he was uncertain of the outcome. That example applies to countless others in the fields of science, technology, literature, exploration, and so on. Hope is the feeling that what is desired is also possible, or that events may turn out for the best.

"Who are you going to believe, me or your lying eyes?"

—Groucho Marx

TWENTY SIX

NEGOTIATION AND DEATH

n her pioneering work with dying patients, Elizabeth Kubler-Ross identified five stages of grief that people go through when faced with the imminent prospect of death, or when faced with any terrible loss or catastrophic event. An analogy may be drawn between everyday negotiation and the five stages of the final negotiation with the prospect of dying so brilliantly described by Kubler-Ross.

When a person knows the end is imminent, a process occurs that bears a striking resemblance to everyday negotiations we see in mediation practice. Kubler-Ross describes five distinct stages.

STAGE 1: DENIAL (OPENING)

The first stage of opposing parties confronting each other is Denial, which is also the first reaction of a person facing death. People do not want to die, and the mind simply denies it.

For plaintiffs in a dispute, the denial often takes the form of unrealistic or illusory expectations, which is a denial of the reality of their situation. A person who has been hurt may carry that wound or grievance from the past into the present, and it can take on a life of its own.

Yet there are two sides to every story. A victim cannot be compensated unless there is someone to pay the compensation; that "someone" also has something to say about what happened. The "de minimis" phenomenon comes into play; the victim minimizes or explains away anything that might be said on behalf of the other side while denying any part of responsibility for the incident. This stage corresponds to the reaction of a patient on being told that she has terminal cancer and has but a short time to live; it is too overwhelming, and the patient goes into denial.

The form of denial taken by the defendant is often a straight-out denial that it ever happened. One sees this in criminal cases, where suspects attempt to construct a hierarchy of defenses—"It wasn't me," "I might have been present but I had nothing to do with it," "I don't even own a gun," "I have a gun but only for self-defense," and so on, as that suspect is confronted with more and more incriminating evidence.

In civil cases, defendants are apt to start with a blanket denial, relying on the legal rule that a plaintiff "has the burden" of proving her case. Following the straight denial, the defendant will construct a hierarchy of defenses that can be lengthy. The primary denial of the alleged perpetrator is the exact opposite of the primary denial of the alleged victim; the defense minimizes its role and explains it away, whereas the plaintiff emphasizes the hurt and seeks to lay all responsibility on the defendant.

STAGE 2: ANGER (COMMUNICATION)

The second stage is Anger. This stage is reached when some of the plaintiff's expectations are dashed and some of the defendant's defenses are breached. At that point the plaintiff becomes angry in a generalized way, but particularly at the defendant for not stepping up to the plate and admitting responsibility, whereas the defendant becomes angry at being unfairly embroiled in the clutches of the legal system. That stage of anger can start at any time, and it can persist throughout the proceeding, but if the matter is to progress by way of negotiation rather than conflict or trial, at some point the third stage must be reached, and the third stage is bargaining.

Anger is an expression of emotion. It naturally follows Denial, which is a suppression of reality. When a part of the reality of the situation is accepted, the parties feel anger that this should have happened to them. However, unless they intend to stay angry forever—and some do in conflicts large and small—at some point the third stage must be entered, which is Bargaining.

STAGE 3: BARGAINING (NEGOTIATION)

Once the parties have put aside enough of their anger, the bargaining stage is reached, at which point the parties can be expected to talk at least with the mediator if not with each other. Having gone through denial and anger, and even if both the denial and the anger are still present, sufficient reality has seeped into the situation that the parties are willing to talk to someone in an attempt to get it resolved.

Mediators have the experience of parties spending a lot of time talking about the matter before they are willing to enter into any kind of serious negotiation, and this can take many forms, but the commonality among all those forms is unreality, which is a refusal to view the situation as a bilateral situation that can be resolved only by taking both sides into account, and that stage is similar to the stages of denial and anger.

STAGE 4: DEPRESSION (IMPASSE)

The fourth stage in the Kubler-Ross sequence is called Depression, which is the state that describes the feeling of defeat, apathy, and impasse—a feeling that the other side is being completely unreasonable and the entire negotiation a waste of time, a feeling that one wants to walk out. These are the moments when the parties feel they ran smack into a brick wall, which is often accompanied by a sense of frustration or defeat or urge to end the whole thing.

These are the times when the mediator must show her mettle, because the reason the parties came to a mediator in the first place instead of working it out between themselves is precisely at these moments. If the mediator has been able to establish trust and presence with the parties, and the empathy with which the mediator is prepared to accept and understand the viewpoint of each party, makes progress possible. If the mediator is able to keep the parties willing to work through the impasse, she is a true professional.

STAGE 5: ACCEPTANCE (CLOSURE)

A mediated negotiation may cycle through the various stages of denial, anger, bargaining, and depression many times during the course of the mediation. No doubt during the final negotiation with death that all of us must go through sometime, there may also be time to cycle many times through those four stages.

The fifth and final stage in the Kubler-Ross sequence is Acceptance, which corresponds with Closure. Acceptance is an acknowledgment that things are as they are and not necessarily what we wish them to be. Closure represents acknowledgment of the reality of the situation.

Kubler-Ross describes acceptance of the inevitability of death as always healing, and closure too is often experienced as healing. Closure results in finality with respect to the given dispute—it may also mean the loss of illusions, the dashing of many hopes, and the failure of expectations and of defenses and represents the necessary coming together of the parties on some kind of middle ground.

In spite of all that, the closure that ends a mediated negotiation also represents a regaining of life energy for parties who had been up to this point entangled in conflict. The conclusion of a mediation means that the parties are now free to move on with their lives. Whether or not they are happy in the moment with the result that they may have felt compelled by circumstances to accept, at least when they wake up the next morning they do not have to worry about this conflict, and conflicts take an enormous amount of energy. Conflicts are expensive in terms of financial resources, time resources, and psychological resources.

A successful mediation is both death and rebirth, as the mediator facilitates the disputants through the stages of denial, anger, bargaining, and depression to acceptance. Acceptance means closure; usually it is a good feeling.

SUMMARY

The five stages of mediation and the five stages of the Kubler-Ross death negotiation correspond as follows: Convening with denial, Opening with anger, Negotiation with bargaining, Impasse with depression, and finally Closure with acceptance.

Life prepares us for death in many ways: entanglement in conflict is one such way. Kubler-Ross shows us the sequence that accompanies knowledge of imminent death; a dying person needs help at such a time. Every negotiation is a petit mort and a chance also for growth; disputants need help at such a time. This is what mediators do.

TWENTY SEVEN
LEVERS OF INFLUENCE

In Robert Cialdini's book *Pre-Suasion: A Revolutionary Way to Influence and Persuade,* the author identifies six principles of persuasion: Affinity (liking), Authority, Consensus, Consistency, Reciprocity, and Scarcity.

To be effective, the mediator must be able to exert some degree of influence, persuasion, and authority. Although the transformative and facilitative schools of mediation seek to intervene in the process to the minimal extent possible, it will be found that even the transformative mediator is exercising the principles of persuasion to help her clients.

In the mediation of litigated cases, parties often use retired judges, and the reason is very simple. A retired judge has authority. It is easier for a corporation or insurance company or firm of attorneys to turn to a retired judge, because at a certain point in the mediation they will able to turn to their clients and say, "The judge thinks this, the judge thinks that."

The subject of persuasion impacts directly into questions of ethics. This question cannot be avoided by denying one's self the use of the principles of persuasion, because that in itself is a decision leading to a course of action. Ethics is the subject of right and wrong actions, and the decision not to act is as much an ethical decision as the decision to act.

A sick person seeking a doctor wants to find a physician with experience, with confidence, with authority, and someone on whom they can place reliance. Anyone with a legal problem wants to find a lawyer who knows what she is talking about, a person with authority. People seeking help want to find someone who is persuasive, authoritative.

Affinity:

Affinity or liking is a principle known to every trial lawyer: Juries give money to lawyers they like and to plaintiffs they like or with whom they feel empathy. Bill Clinton was a personable guy, so the public forgave him. Richard Nixon was not and was forced from office. People are attracted to good-looking people, as every beautiful woman or handsome man soon finds out.

Authority:

People tend to rely on persons in authority. It is as simple as that. That's why retired judges are in demand as mediators. That's why Jimmy Carter successfully brokered the peace treaty between Israel and Egypt.

Consensus:

In any social situation, starting in early childhood, people will tend to observe what other people do in order to decide how to act. Cialdini tells a charming story of a child who learned to swim from one day to the next. Why? Because he saw his little friend of the same age swimming, and said to his father, "Well, Tommy can swim, so I can too." That makes building consensus by tiny steps from the very start of the mediation an important task for the mediator. The mediator will seek agreement on seemingly unimportant points in order to start the process that will eventually lead to the "tipping point" that results in a final agreement.

Consistency:

In politics, in negotiations, in life, human beings value consistency very highly. A politician deemed inconsistent in her positions loses credibility very fast. In a negotiation, the surest way to kill the process is to make a demand and then increase it, which will make an offer, and then decrease it, or to make any kind of statement and then contradict it. This is important as well for the mediator. Human beings value consistency in others. That is why politicians almost never change their party affiliation.

Reciprocity:

This is the age-old concept of "tit for tat." It is also called "stick and carrot." It is the fundamental process of negotiation. A small concession is made, and the conceder then waits to see if a concession will be made in return. Cialdini's reciprocity principle states that people feel an obligation to return a favor.

Scarcity:

Retailers use this principle all the time to persuade people to buy. They put items "on sale," making sure that there appears to be a limited quantity. They advertise "one vehicle at this price." It has very often been observed that an item that simply would not sell at a certain price suddenly becomes in demand at twice that price. People value what they think is scarce. The great art dealer Joe Duveen exploited the perceived scarcity of Old Masters by waging a highly successful one-man campaign over a period of 30 years to sell Renaissance paintings to American millionaires in the 1920s and 1930s at astronomical prices. Realtors used this principle to sell undeveloped land: "They're not making any more of it." Negotiators like to exploit this principle by making an offer accompanied by the words: "This offer is good until five o'clock today." The Hunt brothers from Texas tried to corner the world market in silver, which gave them enormous influence for a while until their scheme utterly collapsed. The story of "bubbles" (the South Sea bubble, the Dutch tulip bubble, the dot.com bubble) are stories of manufactured scarcity. "Get in now before it's too late."

SOURCES OF POWER IN NEGOTIATION
APPRECI(iate):

1. Authority (position, title, charisma)
2. Penalties (punishments, sanctions, compulsion)
3. Persistence (commitment, sacrifice)
4. Rewards (money, title, connection, award, respect, acknowledgment)
5. Expertise (information, know-how, solutions)

6. Connection (relationship: family, ethnic, political, business, financial)

SIX R'S FOR CHANGING MINDS AND OVERCOMING RESISTANCE

This section borrows from the book *Changing Minds*. To get people in conflict to cooperate or collaborate sufficiently to settle or resolve their differences, or even achieve reconciliation, it is necessary that they change their minds. The people are in a dispute because they are of two different minds about a particular thing, which is what they are fighting over. People do not change their minds easily. Some people are prepared to be burned at the stake, literally, rather than change their minds or admit to a change of belief. People cling to the artifacts of their own minds with great stubbornness. This is called *resistance*. When a mediator seeks to bring parties together, she will encounter resistance. If there were no resistance, if changing minds was easy, there would be no need for mediators.

The author identifies six R's, which are helpful in assisting people in changing their minds: reason, research, resonance, redescription, rewards, and real-world events.

Reason is employed by way of the use of argument in order to persuade.

Research is used to collect facts, also with the purpose of persuading; often mediation is a conflict between competing facts.

Resonance appeals to the feeling part of the human personality. Does a proposal feel right? Some people rely heavily upon resonance and prefer it to a reasoned and researched position. Orators and advertisers seek a message that will resonate their audience.

Redescription can be profoundly effective. Matters are often expressed in the negative, but when changed into a positive form of expression they convey a completely different and more attractive meaning. Mediations are often a persistent attempt to redescribe the problem to make solutions seem more attractive.

Rewards are an important part of any negotiation and are usually accompanied by penalties. This is often known as the stick and carrot approach.

Real-world events can have the effect of changing parties' perceptions completely. Such events may be quite trivial, such as going out for lunch. After lunch, what was said in the morning and rejected out of hand may, with the benefit of the simple event of several hours passing and a meal, seem much more attractive.

The ever-present problem of the mediator is that parties do not want to budge but, unless there is some change, they start to get impatient. So the job of the mediator is to continue to make some progress so that there is (at least) a perception of movement. This is necessary to keep the parties at the negotiating table. So it is helpful to the mediator to be able to play upon the six R's, developing a facility with each one, to keep the parties going through the process in a productive way. Ultimately, the matter must be resolved, not by the mediator but by the parties themselves. The combined focused attention of their minds is what will accomplish the result that they have come to mediation to achieve. The mediator, by using the six R's, helps to guide the process to its successful conclusion.

TWENTY EIGHT

THIRTY NINE TECHNIQUES FOR OVERCOMING IMPASSE

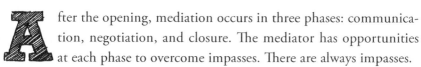fter the opening, mediation occurs in three phases: communication, negotiation, and closure. The mediator has opportunities at each phase to overcome impasses. There are always impasses.

The objective is to move the parties from positions based on consideration of rights and obligations to a different mind-set based on needs and interests. Instead of concentrating on fault, damages, and remedies, which are inherently confrontational, the parties need to focus on their needs and interests.

Here are some techniques that may assist you in accomplishing this task.

1. Risk/benefit analysis

    This mental exercise is the subject of many books and articles, including write-ups on Wikipedia. Everyone older than 20 months of age performs this analysis constantly. Two-year-olds are particularly ruthless. Even dogs perform this analysis. It is standard in any negotiation. However, like all formulations, it is flawed in the sense that it cannot produce a "standard" answer, for the simple reason that assessment of risk is subjective, as it depends on the level of risk a person will accept.

    Here is an example, set in Spain in 1492.

    Christopher Columbus: I think we can get to the China spice trade by going west.

King Ferdinand: Ridiculous; you'll just fall off the edge of the world.

Columbus: We don't think there is an edge; we think it's round.

Queen Isabella: That's not what the Bible says.

Ferdinand: How is that even possible? It's flat, just look out of the window.

Columbus: What's the worst thing that can happen? (WATNA) If I fail, I die, but if we succeed, your Majesties' wealth will be unimaginable.

Ferdinand: Well, we can let you have three ships.

Ferdinand (privately to Isabella): We're only risking three little ships, and if he's right, Spain will rule the world; it's worth the risk.

Isabella: It's only three little ships, and for the glory of God; it's worth the risk.

Christopher (to himself): I will either die, or be famous forever; it's worth the risk.

2. Cost/reward analysis

Here is the kind of statement you can find on the Internet:

"Compute $200 \Sigma \pi i \, p_{ij}$, where π is the limiting distribution computed previously and the sum is taken over all ordered pairs (i,j) such that a player passes Go when moving from state i to state j."

This may mean something to some people, but for our purposes it is sufficient to know that cost/reward analysis is like risk/benefit analysis but used in situations where one just needs to point out that spending $100,000 on a $10,000 case makes no sense.

3. BATNA (Best Alternative to a Negotiated Agreement)

This acronym is used all the time in mediation. Wikipedia has a good article on BATNA. It is used in mediation to get parties to evaluate the alternative to settlement, which is usually trial. Trial is expensive and uncertain; it may be better than settlement, or it may not, and the decision is difficult because it involves uncertainties.

BATNA always refers to the future and tries to evaluate different futures. It is sometimes called WATNA, that is, the worst alternative to a negotiated agreement.

4. FUD (Fear, Uncertainty, and Doubt)

    Some mediators like to frighten parties by instilling in them FUD as to what will happen if they do not settle. It is a heavy-handed approach, but sometimes parties need a reality check.

5. Conditional or virtual movement: "If they do this, then will you do that...?"

    This technique usually works well. It works because parties are often unwilling to move for fear that any movement will be seen as weakness. (Rabbits have the same fears when confronted with snakes.) Using the virtual approach, parties can "move without moving," until they see that the other party will also move. The virtual move then becomes a real move. It is a way of building trust and creating movement.

6. Ranges of numbers

    The purpose of ranges is to get away from the anchoring affect of numbers, and also the emotional effect of numbers.

    Using ranges is often effective. When a plaintiff agrees to a range of 50 to 80, and the defendant agrees to a range of 20 to 40, the mediator sees immediately that the parties are really only 10 apart (50 – 40 = 10). Tip: The plaintiff will always take his or her lower number, and the defendant will always pay his or her higher number, but as they are often not stupid and know about this, they take this into account when stating their ranges, so ranges can be expected to change.

7. Ask the plaintiff, "What is the defendant thinking?" Ask the defendant, "What is the plaintiff thinking?"

    The purpose of asking this is to get parties to recognize that a settlement must always be mutually agreed. Some parties think if their number is 100 and the other side has 20, the settlement must be 100, or vice versa. The point is that there are necessarily at least two parties involved; it is surprising how often one or both parties cannot see this.

8. Brainstorming

    Put any solution or suggestion on the table, no matter how far-fetched it seems. This can help by loosening up people's brains, widening their perspectives, and freeing them from fixed positions.

9. Mediator's proposal

    Experienced mediators often use this technique, and it does take some experience to get it right. When parties are within the Zone of Possible Agreement (ZOPA) but cannot bridge the gap on their own, the mediator may make a proposal to each side. "Are you willing to accept (plaintiff) or pay (defendant) $X to settle this case today?" If both agree, the case is settled. If either or both do not agree, the case is not settled.

10. Look for the missing pieces in the presentation.

    What is omitted gives you the clue to what parties are themselves not seeing, or hiding. They may be hiding stuff from themselves, and "wishing away" their weak points. In the long run, those weak points will usually get exposed, so it helps to do this sooner rather than later.

11. Use the Copernican principle of mediocrity.

    Mediocrity expresses the condition of humans, yet each human believes deep down that he or she is not mediocre but very special. Before Copernicus, it was understood that the heavens revolved around the earth, the center of the universe; humans were indeed special in this worldview. Copernicus, followed by Galileo and Kepler and by now countless others, have shown that the universe is vast beyond our conception and that our planet is just one of multiple billions; we are just not that "special."

    Yet each and every one of us has the sense that we are individually unique and special, and we want to be treated as if we matter and have value. The legal system does not provide this service; indeed, the system (and most other human systems) treat the individual as a "particle on a conveyor belt" to be processed in a uniform way according to the system's rules and needs. This is often upsetting to individuals who are caught in a system that treats them as a number or standardized particle to be processed to the final result, which is "case closed."

Parties who come to mediation with various grievances can be helped by a mediator who can validate a party's uniqueness and allow the party to feel adequately served by a system that is essentially designed to "process" an abundance of claims quite impersonally. So although we live in a Copernican universe, and use a legal system that does not treat people as unique individuals, a good mediator can make an individual feel special and willing to accept an imperfect result that is nonetheless "as good as it gets."

12. Joint session with all participants

13. Joint session with lawyers only

14. Private session with each lawyer separately, or with lawyer plus client

15. Try to convert the lawyers into counselors for their clients' needs and interests, rather than adversarial advocates for their positions.

16. Search for underlying needs and interests. Ask: What do you really need?

17. Suggest numbers where appropriate. It sometimes helps to suggest higher numbers than the plaintiff is demanding when speaking to the plaintiff, and suggest lower numbers than the defendant is offering when speaking to the defendant, to attempt to get them thinking in a less fixed way.

18. There may not be the possibility of resolution on the particular day. This is not actually a settlement technique but sometimes just a statement of reality.

19. Expand the "pie" if possible.

20. Say, "It all sounds good, but do you want to settle this dispute today?"

21. The black box system—do not relay numbers at all. This is hard to do because parties really want to talk numbers, but some mediators manage to practice this technique.

22. If you are really stumped, ask, "What would you do now if you were me?"

23. Ask each side, "What is the other side's next move?" This mimics chess players, who plan ahead as far as they can. The idea is to get opposing parties to prepare mentally a path to resolution.

24. Acknowledge strengths and be willing to point out weaknesses. It is easy to acknowledge strengths but not so easy to point out weaknesses in a way that will be accepted.

25. Ask for movement.

    Here's the magic phrase: "Please move." Do not say: "Or I'll shoot your goldfish."

26. Trash and bash

    This is the lowest common denominator of a mediator's skill or want of it. It involves "trashing" a party's case and "bashing" the party or the lawyer for good measure. Does it work? Yes, it does work sometimes, but it is crude.

27. Educate plaintiff's attorney on the tactical value of not starting way beyond his or her intended target and the defense on not starting way below his or her intended target. This may require some delicacy, but parties often do not appreciate the mediator telling them how to negotiate.

28. Allay defendant's fears of having "no room to move."

    This is a common fear of defendants, who want plaintiffs to accept what the defense has to offer. If the defense gets too close to its best and final number, whereas the plaintiff is still very far from that number, defendants worry that they have lost any further persuasive power. Yet at some point the defense must get to its final number, so it is really a matter of timing. The mediator cannot push parties further than they are willing to go at that moment but still must keep the process moving.

29. Defendant agrees to pay mediator's fee.

    A defendant will sometimes pay the entire mediation fee to close the deal at the defendant's number. This is because that money comes out of a different account. The mediator's fee is low compared with the settlement number, but it can often make the difference between settlement and stalemate.

30. Toss a coin or draw straws.

    The author has done this twice, but it is uncommon and hardly to be recommended as a general practice.

31. Coach everyone.

    Many people, including attorneys, will mess up the deal if they get the chance of speaking face-to-face with their opponent. The fact that we call that person the "opponent" is indicative of the mind-set.

32. Politeness, attentiveness, and charm go a long way.

    It really helps to be civilized, especially toward other humans. Corporations are fictional entities but are always represented by humans. Anyone can be polite and attentive, even if charm is too challenging.

33. Always follow up if the matter does not settle on the day.

    This is critical. Always follow up. A great many cases settle in the week following mediation, but the mediator has to follow up.

34. Find the point(s) of resistance.

    What is really holding a party to a fixed position? Ask them why. The "point of resistance" may surprise you. Car salesmen are good at this.

35. If you can't go the extra inch, better to sign the deal with a twenty-four-hour back-out period than not sign anything and agree to meet again.

Parties who have signed with a twenty-four-hour back-out clause are far more likely to accept the agreement, having slept on it, than if they walk out with no agreement and nothing more than a promise to meet again.

36. First, list various possible events that might occur. Second, consider the costs or gains associated with each possibility. Third, discount each possibility by its probability—estimated likelihood that it will occur. Finally, evaluate the overall picture by multiplying each possibility by its probability.

37. Neutral evaluation

This is an assessment of the dispute as to the likely outcome, performed by a neutral outsider. Judges often do this as they have some credibility.

38. Reality testing

Questions about likelihood of prevailing, contrary factual information, direct costs of litigation, and indirect costs of litigation.

39. Apology

Wonderful, but if the person who apologizes wants something in return for the apology, it is worthless. Apologies must be "no strings attached," which is quite rare.

TWENTY NINE

THE HEART AS AN ORGAN OF PERCEPTION

Where do we begin? Begin with the heart.

- Dame Julian of Norwich,

c1400 A.D

Does a mediator need a heart? That depends on what you think a heart is for. Around the time the *Mayflower* set sail (1620) from Plymouth in England bound for the new world, the great Dr. Harvey made the discovery in London that the heart functions as a pump for blood. Until then, the teachings of the Roman physician known to us as Galen, who taught that the blood moved with a kind of pulse or wave motion, had been treated as the established orthodoxy for more than fourteen hundred years. Harvey's discovery aroused such consternation and hostility that one eminent physician remarked that he "would rather be wrong with Galen than be right with Harvey."

Ironically, modern research tells us that the heart is incapable of pumping blood through the miles of blood vessels in a human body, many tinier than a human hair. Certainly, the heart muscle functions as a powerful pump, capable of throwing a jet of water vertically ten feet into the air, but to pump two gallons of blood per minute through thousands of miles of blood vessels is estimated to require a pump capable of throwing a fifty-kilo weight a mile into the air.

Further, Dr. Harvey knew nothing about electromagnetism, but today we know that the heart emits powerful electromagnetic impulses with every heartbeat and is by far the most powerful such transmitter in the human body. For example, it is in this capacity five thousand times more powerful than the brain.

Shortly after conception, the collection of cells that make up the beginnings of an embryo begin to pulsate, and those pulsations are electromagnetic. When two electromagnetic emitters come into contact with each other, their fields of energy interfere with each other and that interference is recognizable because it interferes with the wave patterns. This is the principle upon which a host of modern communication devices rely—for example, radar, sonar, and cell phones. Cell phones rely upon microwave transmissions, but the principle is the same. The receiving organ picks up the transmission of the emitting organ and interprets it as a communication. Sound waves in the form of human speech are converted into microwaves that are sent from transmitter to transmitter and then converted back into sound waves to be received by a human ear, and the human brain then interprets those noises as speech having a certain meaning.

The developing heart functions the same way. The developing embryo perceives nothing but the steady heartbeat of its mother. The embryonic heart develops long before the embryonic ear, which hears first only the rush of blood, but the developing embryo starts to interpret the mother's heartbeats, and those electromagnetic transmissions are interpreted as emotions. The four principal emotions are sad, mad, glad, and scared, just as the four basic tastes are sweet, sour, bitter, and salt, but from these simple bases we combine and interpret an enormous range of information. We can affirm that the heart is an organ for pumping blood but also a transmitter and interpreter of emotional states.

Although our science has been slow to recognize the heart as an organ of feeling and perception, our language is in no doubt. Consider the plethora of heart-based expressions in English usage: heartfelt, from the bottom of my heart, I wish with all my heart, with heart and soul, heart-stricken, heart-sick, heart-rending decision, heavy-hearted, lighthearted, with an innocent heart, a black-hearted villain, the heart has its reasons that reason cannot comprehend, our hearts are joined as one, I heartily agree, and so on. And we talk about hunches, female intuition, and gut instinct.

When we consider our role as mediators, we must wonder what we can bring to the table that the parties do not already possess for themselves. We usually provide a space for them to sit and a cup of coffee, but then what? Some of us may offer suggestions, but can all of us say that we are likely to prove better problem-solvers than the parties themselves? Often parties are represented by attorneys, who are trained problem-solvers, and everyone present in the room knows a hundred times as much as the mediator will ever know. They have often been living with their mutual problem for a long time, and the files they have built up are voluminous.

The mediator is not asked to read those files from beginning to end. The mediator can have no more than a rudimentary knowledge of the details of the dispute in which the parties have been engaged for so long. It is a little presumptuous to expect that the mediator can read a brief, listen to the various communications for several hours, and come up with a satisfactory solution, and indeed we do not do so. We expect the parties to resolve their own dispute, and we claim to be "facilitating" the process or providing a "safe space" in which they can interact.

But what does it mean to provide a safe space? They could as easily go to a hotel and sit in the lobby, or meet at the courthouse, which is protected by armed guards. I suggest that what makes our space "safe" is the influence of our own personality and our own personal ability to help each party think or feel their way toward a mutually satisfactory conclusion. Of course, I do not say that it is simply a matter of breathing deeply and smiling. Our mediator mind is also engaged, but our society is not lacking in problem-solving ability. It is lacking in heart. As a culture, our hearts are uneasy, which is why diseases of the heart are the commonest cause of death. Perhaps this is the reason why mediation exists at all as a profession. It is to provide something that in our present society is in short supply.

THIRTY

NO WAY OUT: THE PRISONER'S DILEMMA

T he prisoner's dilemma is often expressed as a game played on a computer, but we see the ramifications of the prisoner's dilemma in all aspects of living in society. The essential question asked by the prisoner's dilemma is, Can people be naturally cooperative, or do our individual genes require a selfish response to life situations? This question is of interest to mediators, as variations of it are played out in all mediations.

The crux of the argument that individuals are essentially motivated by self-interest is expressed in the famous statement of Thomas Hobbes—life is "a war of all against all." Hobbes had a bleak view of human existence, because he saw the war of all against all as the natural state of mankind, with no other natural outcome but, as he put it, "the life of man, solitary, poor, nasty, brutish and short." The same idea is expressed in the statement attributed to Heraclitus 2,500 years ago: "War is the father and ruler of all things."

The acceptance of this condition has justified for centuries our systems of laws and hierarchies of authority, to counteract the natural tendency of human beings to revert into the anarchic state described by Hobbes. The view of man as essentially self-interested also finds support in the great work of Adam Smith, *Wealth of Nations*, published the same year as the Declaration of Independence. In it, Smith takes the view that each person is motivated by self-interest yet postulates that in a society based on "natural liberty," even though each individual in society pursues his own rational self-interest, the results will be beneficial for the commonwealth as a whole, as though the vast workings of countless individuals pursing self-interest were regulated by an invisible hand.

Further support for the view that human beings are essentially motivated by self-interest is found in modern studies on genetics. The modern view is that human beings are motivated by a desire to propagate their own individual genes and that there is nothing in the genetic makeup of human beings that points to any kind of evolution of a cooperative gene. (See Dawkins: *The Selfish Gene*; but see Ridley: *The Origins of Virtue*, for a different perspective.)

Gene or no gene, many people are uncomfortable with the idea that we are fundamentally selfish, and although when Adam Smith was writing in the second half of the eighteenth century the idea of an invisible hand may have seemed attractive, today in our more rigorously scientific civilization we are not willing to accept the idea of such a hand mysteriously regulating our affairs to ensure that, in spite of our individual selfishness, everything comes out all right in the end. Yet, on the other hand, our daily experience in living is one of cooperation as well as competition, and the theory of the selfish gene does not appear able to account for the observed and experienced reality that we are also cooperative beings.

Some social scientists have sought to use the power of computers to find a way out of the prisoner's dilemma—to find a formula pursuant to which it is always better to cooperate—because of discomfort with the idea that we are prisoners of the imperatives of our own genes.

The prisoner's dilemma can be expressed positively and negatively. It is expressed negatively for prisoners caught by the police. The two prisoners are regarded as having an option of whether to cooperate with each other, by not talking to the police, or whether to defect from each other and start cooperating with police. One should bear in mind that the first one to talk routinely gets a better deal from prosecuting authorities than suspects who stay silent.

So this is not just a computer game; it is something that police suspects are forced to experience every time they get caught with fellow suspects. In the version that is usually taught, and played on computers, the two prisoners are offered the following choices: If they cooperate with each other (i.e., stay silent), each will be sentenced on a lesser charge to one year in jail, and this is called the reward, the reward for cooperation with each other. If they both choose to defect (i.e., they both talk to the police), then they each get three years in jail.

So at this point it is easy to see that it is better to cooperate than to defect. But they are in different rooms, with no means of communicating. The game, which for many is a reality, becomes more interesting when one cooperates and the other defects. In this instance, the first to defect (i.e., talk to the police) gets off free by testifying against the coconspirator. This is called the *temptation*.

The second prisoner, who refuses to cooperate (i.e., stays silent), gets five years, which is called sucker's payoff. In real life, often the temptation to get off free is available only to the first person to defect, and so both suspects are faced with the temptation and pressure to be the first to defect. You have the choice of being a rat or a sucker, but if a rat, you need to be first.

This game can also be played for positive points, in which the numbers are simply reversed. The cooperators with each other get three points, which is their reward for cooperating. The defectors get one point each, which is their punishment for defecting. If one cooperates and the other defects, the cooperator gets the sucker's payoff (zero points) and the defector gets five points, which is the temptation.

Expressed in this mathematical way, it is obvious that in every case it is better to defect than to cooperate, even though it may seem that cooperation is the better course. The reason it is better to defect is clear simply by adding up the numbers. If you always defect, the maximum number of points you can get is six—one point if both defect, five points if only you defect—but if you always cooperate, the maximum number of points you ever can get is three.

So unless you know in advance what the other person is going to do, the only safe course of action is to choose defection. This is the prisoner's dilemma. If you alter the numbers (i.e., ten points for cooperation), then of course everyone would always cooperate, but the experience of life is that cooperation produces slower but more certain long-term gain but defection works better in the short run.

The prisoner's dilemma arises because of lack of communication. If the parties to the game or problem are perfectly synchronized with each other, they will see that, if playing the game over and over again, cooperation will result in a better outcome over the long run—thus the mafia law of silence. But the temptation to obtain a short-term advantage is always present, and the difficulty of obtaining the level of trust necessary to achieve cooperation is always present as well.

Where two people are involved, say man and wife or two partners, a high level of cooperation may be achieved. What if there are fifteen people? The matter becomes exponentially more problematic. What if five hundred people are involved, or a small town, or a large country? How does one achieve cooperation on that kind of scale? It is a basic problem of civilization. When we get into very large numbers involving populations, one sees how immensely difficult it is to achieve the benefits of cooperation versus short-term benefits of pursuing one's own narrow interest.

That is why the saying goes that all politics are local, but this is another way of saying when it comes right down to it, people will vote their own immediate interests, people will vote their pocketbooks, people will vote what is good for them personally in their particular small sphere, rather than looking at the rest of the country, or the world, as a whole.

Obviously, this has immediate practical ramifications for mediators, because the challenge is always to get disputing parties to reach a level of cooperation so that they can achieve settlement.

There are lots of versions of the prisoner's dilemma. One is called the "wolf's dilemma," first suggested by Hofstadter, in which a number of people are separated, each with their finger on a button, and the game is this: The first person to push the button gets $100 and everyone else gets nothing, but if each person sits without pushing the button for a given period of time, say 20 minutes, they each get $500. The dilemma here is again one of trust. The temptation to defect is made less appealing because the temptation to cooperate is five times as attractive, provided one can be certain that no one else is going to get the certain, though lesser, money by pushing the button first.

Social scientists have been playing with the prisoner's dilemma for many years, and their efforts have intensified since the wide introduction of personal computers. One of the original realizations was that prisoners' dilemmas in one form or another are experienced in daily life.

Any situation in which you can cut an immediate deal for yourself, and yet if you know everyone else is going to cooperate that it would be better, is a prisoner's dilemma. Another way of experiencing it is to realize that if everyone acts for herself, the results will be very much worse than if people cooperated, and yet there is still the temptation to be one of the (few) winners rather than one of the (many) suckers.

An example sometimes given is that if everyone could be trusted not to steal cars or rob department stores, then insurance rates would be cheaper for everyone, costs would go down, the general benefit for all would be increased. And yet it does not take too many defectors to create a situation in which everyone has to lock their cars, in which department stores have to have security guards with the corresponding increase in the cost of goods.

The prisoner's dilemma is experienced on a continuous basis with respect to our environment. Overfishing is an enormous problem, or the extinction of species, or the overgrowing of crops, or cutting down the rain forest—all of these produce immediate gain for the persons doing it but an overall loss for everyone else. If anyone could be sure that other people would not be selfish, then one might forgo individualism for which collectively they pay a heavy price.

Yet we live in a society in which individualism is prized as an ultimate value. This has been called the "tragedy of the commons"—the "commons" succeeds only if no one abuses it, and it is nearly always abused. The effort of some political philosophies is to develop systems in which self-interest can somehow be made to produce a favorable result for the common interest.

On a macrolevel, one can see that communism was a utopian attempt to create a society in which, as expressed in the *Communist Manifesto*, each gives according to his ability and each receives according to his need. That utopian vision elevates cooperation as a supreme value, but in practice, as we all know, it failed utterly. Why? Because "some are more equal than others"; the bosses stole everything.

Capitalism can be seen as an attempt to acknowledge that each individual is motivated by self-interest and yet to create a system in which the common good can also be preserved. Yet experience has shown that unrestrained capitalism can lead to monopoly and oppression. There is no substitute for balance, and the balance is between cooperation and competition.

One of the chief variables in any system is time. Often there is tension or conflict between short-term and long-term interest. It is very well to live in a society devoted to consumption, but if in doing so one sacrifices one's children's education, which requires large capital investment and long-term vision, then the outcome two to three generations hence will be poor.

Scientists and mathematicians have sought to use computers and computer games to find a computerized, mathematical solution out of the bleak conclusion of the prisoner's dilemma that selfishness is the only rational option for a human being.

The prisoner's dilemma may be regarded as a branch of game theory. Game theory seeks to discover strategies for success in which the best option depends upon what other people do, in circumstances where it may not be easy to know in advance what anyone else is going to do.

The goal of game theory is to find a formula, a strategy that will work in all circumstances, even though the variable is what other people in the situation will do. Mathematician John Nash won a Nobel Prize for developing the Nash Equilibrium, which is a mathematical way of expressing the optimal response to what other people are doing or going to do, even though that optimal response may not be entirely satisfactory. In other words, the Nash Equilibrium often requires one to make the best of poor circumstances, and this very often occurs in the negotiation situation where one of the parties is in a weak position.

Consider, for example, a game invented by Hammerstein and Selten, in which A and B must share a given sum of money with each other. A gets to play first, and he needs to decide whether the money will be shared equally or whether he will take the larger share. B plays second, and he must decide on the total amount of money that will be shared. Thus, A chooses the split, and B chooses the total amount. The second rule is that if A chooses a 50:50 split, he gets half and B gets half but, incredibly unfairly, if A does not share the money equally, he gets his split—say, 90:10—multiplied by ten times.

Unfairness pays big for A, provided B behaves rationally and chooses not to punish A for being unfair. If A decides to take a larger share, he is then at the mercy of B, who decides the amount of the total pot to be shared. There is nothing B can do about it once A has chosen to take the larger share. What is the rational thing for B to do? On the one hand, he may want to stick it to A for being unfair but, if he does, he punishes himself as well as A. B's rational choice is to choose the largest possible sum of money, because thereby he gets more, even though it grates on him that A has behaved in this way.

This is the Nash Equilibrium—for A to play unfair and for B to play high. This is not the perfect outcome for B, because he must put up with the emotional anguish of seeing A succeed, but rationally it is the best of a bad job. However, as we all know in practice, in numerous instances people will not choose the rational option but will prefer a revenge option based on emotion.

When the prisoner's dilemma is played between two people a great many times on a computer, it is found that they prove to be very willing to cooperate. Even though they see the advantage in making a quick killing at the other's expense, where they knew that they were going to play again and again, the value of cooperation outweighs the value of a quick advantage.

Cooperation pays in the long term, which is how societies hold together over time. Yet in many circumstances in modern life, we are not playing the same game over and over with the same people. Particularly in mediation, we are playing with someone whom we are never going to see again, and the temptation not to cooperate is very great, and this is a bias that in almost every situation the mediator needs to overcome. The challenge is always how to get this pair of people or group of people to cooperate long enough to get this particular situation resolved.

The search of the computer scientists to find a stable strategy, in which the advantages of playing that strategy always produce a viable result whether or not anyone else in the game is playing a different strategy, proved in practice to be exceedingly difficult, leading eventually to the conclusion that there is no foolproof formula.

A biologist named John Maynard Smith wanted to find out why, in the wild, animals generally do not fight to the death. They tend to choose other strategies, such as to submit or to leave the scene. Smith invented a game that he called Hawk and Dove, in which the hawk corresponds to the defector in the prisoner's dilemma and the dove corresponds to the cooperator.

If hawk meets dove, hawk wins, but if hawk meets another hawk, hawk can be badly wounded. This is important in the wild, because animals that are badly wounded have a poor survival prognosis. Although hawk always beats dove, if dove meets dove then the outcome is positive, but more interesting, if dove meets hawk over and over again, then the qualities of dove start to improve dove's chances, particularly if dove can learn to change from dove to hawk when the occasion demands—such a dove is called a "retaliator," and in other contexts a "shape shifter."

When social scientists started playing the prisoner's dilemma on computers, they discovered something surprising. Computers, which are entirely rational, started cooperating in circumstances in which it seemed irrational. In 1979, Robert Axelrod, a political scientist, asked for submissions of a number of programs in circumstances in which each program would play another program numerous times, and he set it up so that it would be possible to determine which program produced the winning strategy. The astonishing thing was that the cooperative programs tended to do well, and the winner was the simplest and most cooperative of all.

The simplest and most cooperative of all the submitted programs won the tournament. It was submitted by a Canadian political scientist named Anatol Rapoport, who submitted a program called Tit-for-Tat. Tit-for-Tat starts cooperatively, and then simply follows what the other person did last time. In other words, if cooperation is met by defection or aggression, then Rapoport's program will retaliate. But if cooperation is met by cooperation, then the Rapoport program continues to cooperate. So whereas the habitual cooperator is likely to get thwarted, the cooperator who is willing to turn into a retaliator—that is, a dove that is willing to turn into a hawk and then back into a dove—wins the game.

The first time Axelrod attempted this tournament, fourteen programs were submitted, with Tit-for-Tat the winner. The second time Axelrod set up the tournament, sixty-two programs were submitted and, once again, Tit-for-Tat proved to be the winner. Axelrod wrote a book on the subject, in which he identified Tit-for-Tat's four essential attributes resulting in its overall success: (1) It was cooperative, but (2) willing to retaliate. (3) If after retaliation the opponent started to cooperate, then Tit-for-Tat was forgiving. (4) Finally, it communicated by its actions a clear and consistent message. In this way, Tit-for-Tat has the best chance of eliciting not only long-term cooperation but short-term cooperation as well—its strategy is cooperative, retaliatory, forgiving, clear, and consistent.

The reason that Tit-for-Tat's strategy has a better chance of success, although not foolproof, is that hawks tend to kill each other off. So, although at first the hawks tend to kill the doves, hawks that never learn to be nice eventually always come up against a faster gun and get shot down. This can happen to anyone, but the advantage of flexibility in the long run, and even in the short run, is overwhelming. It doesn't pay to hope that life is different than what we actually experience. We cannot always be peacemakers, nor can we always win by being warriors. We have to learn to be flexible.

However, Tit-for-Tat cannot be a universal panacea. If there were a universal panacea, we would have discovered or evolved into it by now. Everyone knows the expression "tit-for-tat" killings. In other words, if a cooperative move is met by a retaliatory move, then tit-for-tat demands that the next move by the cooperator be one of retaliation. But then if the player on the other side retaliates to the retaliation, the game spirals downward out of control into what amounts to a blood feud. The danger of tit-for-tat is that it can lead to mutual recrimination or retaliation, from which there is no escape, and we observe this in current events as well as historically, and we observe this in mediation.

The social scientists with their computer games have established that the dilemma all must experience in their own lives, between the survival imperatives of the individual and the survival interests of society, is not subject to an invariably winning formula. It is a form of tension or strife that is part of our condition. We are genetically programmed for individual survival, but we know from experience, personal and historical, that we need each other.

It is lucky for mediators that no formula exists. If there were a formula, mediators would be redundant. Negotiating parties seek their own self-interest. They are obliged to cooperate because cooperation, in the particular circumstances, is in their self-interest, but they wish to cooperate to the minimal extent required by the circumstances. Hence the "dance" for advantage, and that is why mediators can be useful. The parties cannot escape the dilemma; all they can do is try to maximize whatever advantages they possess vis-à-vis the others in the negotiation. It is not patty cake; it is war waged with kisses.

THIRTY ONE

MEDIATION VIGNETTES

ollowing are some cases. Identifying details have been altered to protect confidentiality.

CLASS ACTION

Case on appeal on issue of attorney fees and costs. The underlying case had settled for $15 million. The class plaintiff's attorney, following usual practice, then filed a motion for attorney fees and costs. The court awarded $5 million to come out of the plaintiff's award. Plaintiffs appealed on the basis that the court should have made a separate award against defendants for fees and costs, leaving the principal settlement amount intact for distribution among the class. The dispute went to mediation.

Course of negotiation:

Plaintiffs demand $4 million from defendants.

Defendants offer $675,000.

Plaintiff drops to $3.10 million.

Defendant counters with $1.125 million.

Both sides agree to hear a mediator proposal.

Mediator proposal is $2.0 million.

Parties taste grief, feel pain, accept the proposal.

Elapsed time: 11 hours

Practice comment: Very big gap to close in one leap. But it worked; perhaps it helped that it was getting late and the air-conditioning had been turned off.

Practice comment: Defendants threatened to walk out several times. Couple of times I mollified them and the final time I just said flatly they weren't leaving.

Practice comment: Defense attorney clever but complicated; started every other sentence with "The problem is…" This makes it very difficult for the mediator. So I took the chief defendant decision-maker into a separate room to chat, and he sounded pretty good. Then I got the plaintiff attorney. Things were proceeding productively, but then defense attorney came in and was outraged, both because I was speaking with his client without him, and also because I had then included the plaintiff attorney. He felt it put him in a bad light and he had a good point so I apologized very profusely and went on apologizing. However, the tactic broke the deadlock, and the case got settled.

FIGHTS IN PARADISE

Homeowners Association (HOA) mediations are grueling. HOAs are like miniaturized banana republics. Dictators on one side; guerillas on the other. Suppression of dissent. Favors to friends. Midnight phone calls. The call to arms. Surprise assaults and ruined expectations, boiling resentment, and finally the lawsuit no one can afford.

The legal issues in these cases are always an interpretation of the governing documents and the alleged failure of the board to perform its fiduciary responsibilities. The real issues are always personal—very personal. What makes them grueling are the numbers. This one was five board members on one side and three outraged owners on the other. That's eight plus two attorneys who have run up quite some bills, which means quite a bit of posturing for the clients before we can get down to business. They are all different, and the upset of each individual has to be handled personally.

What keeps a fight going is usually that one association member, not on the board, gets driven to obsession. That member starts investigating, asks for documents and doesn't get them, goes to great lengths to build up a large dossier, interviews officials, attends every board meeting, and finally gets a lawyer. The board feels besieged and clams up and, if the HOA carries insurance, refers the matter to their carrier. Carriers defend these under a reservation of rights, which means they will defend the case but won't foot the bill for an adverse judgment, so it's not a free ride for the defendants.

In this case, a large number of "issues" were unearthed, but they all boiled down to hurt feelings on both sides and mutual lack of transparency. The plaintiffs had a great deal to say and a list of nine demands plus fees. The defendants also had a lot to say but eventually agreed to all the demands. I left the fees until the end because, if all other issues are resolved, it's harder to blow up the settlement on the single issue of fees. The fees were actually minimal, and the negotiation went like this, in the ninth hour: demand 15, offer 5, demand 10, offer 7.5, agreed and settled. The only hard part about this simple part was the loud objections of board members, who didn't "want to reward bad behavior," "this is a bad precedent," all those kinds of comments, even though the carrier was paying.

As for the issues, there was little substantive. Because the plaintiffs felt they were not being heard, they filed suit. Because the defendants felt they were being attacked, they defended. The suit was to force communication. It is nearly impossible to get to the bottom of these fights, and fortunately, it isn't necessary. It's only necessary to defuse the situation, which in practical terms means absorbing all the grievances on one side and all the aggrieved defensiveness on the other. Exactly how this is done is hard to describe because it's hard to observe oneself and do it at the same time. The student observer who was present takes up the story from here.

Student observer: You immediately separated both sides out. We went into the more contentious (plaintiff) room first, which was two women suing their home association. They came with their attorney, who was also positioned to be quite bulldoggish and aggressive on their behalf. One woman was with her husband.

We went into that room first. We were there for over an hour. During this time, they spent the preponderance of the time telling you about another lawsuit that had happened, and what happened during it and why they were so unhappy with the board members. They spoke very little about the actual case, the actual issues, or the actual trial that was coming up. They really just vented their unhappiness, mostly about the fire hazard in the area and showed pictures. During this time, you said little except for asking for some clarifying points, and their attorney did quite a bit of posturing and showed he was the attorney. You said almost nothing.

Then we went into the other room an hour later, and spoke with the five Board members and their attorney. You basically told them you wanted them to act with consistency and impartiality. You highlighted as well to them, of course, they wanted consistency and impartiality too, and they all nodded. Then you mentioned the fire hazard, and said of course everyone has the same concern to guard against fire, and you went down the list of complaints basically assuming they would agree and they did—it seemed very simple—but also you gave them their chance to vent. Their attorney very cleverly said almost nothing except for her own unhappiness with the fact that they were in this room at all; she vented that point several times during the day.

Unlike the other room where you basically were quiet and let them say anything, in this room you pointed out whether their points were valid or invalid, and where they were in fact complaining or had personal issues. You didn't give them the huge arena of gripe that you gave the other room, but even so we were there for almost an hour.

And then we went back into the other room and you started to get very on point, two hours in, which involved starting to go back into the past, but you started to use the pictures and the map to keep them very focused. As you pointed out, that was then and this is now, and please just show me that on the map, you also told them basically the board, the defendants, wants what you want and agree to most of your demands. But the plaintiffs lamented having been through all that before and so they started to vent about what happened at the actual meetings of the Association. "They told us to shut up and sit down," exclaimed some of the plaintiffs, which was verified by their attorney. And that's when you started to put in a bit more control. And that's when you said I know I wasn't there, but I'm here now and they are definitely communicating, so let's work toward resolution now.

Because it was a valid point and well taken, the attorney started working in the direction of settlement. Just before lunch, you handled the most vocal and aggressive plaintiff. Just as she finished quite a really forceful speech, you were looking right in her eye and explained that while she's articulate, well researched, and intelligent, no one could receive what she's saying for how she's saying it. Her husband was laughing, amazed, and seemed very grateful that you'd said those words to her. She was laughing too and agreed. Then you sent them, plaintiffs, all out for lunch.

From there, we went into the other room with the defendants and had lunch brought in, so we worked through lunch. You started to tell them specifically, these are the things you've decided that are now agreed upon, and they kind of just went along with it. First you dealt with the procedure items like consistency, impartiality, transparency, and fairness; then we talked about the four specific items the plaintiffs had brought up, which were the trailer, the stairs, the landscaping, and that piece of land. You talked about the specifics of that, and you found out they didn't even know about the stairs. The trailer was on the guy's property, not on common ground, but the board members were very conciliatory toward him at this point, because his house had been burned down. Finally you very pointedly asked if they were willing to go to trial for his illegal trailer, and they decided they were not. That was after lunch, though. So there was about an hour and a half of going over each of these four issues. Then you told them you were going to bring the plaintiffs in, and everyone's eyes went quite wide.

You specifically told them how they were going to act when the other people came into the room. There'd be no eye rolling, there'd be no talking except what they were assigned to say, and there would, in fact, be quite a bit of sucking it up. You even used those words, "Suck it up." And then you left the attorney to work with them.

We went to the other room. Then you instructed the other room on how—exactly how they would behave. Then you said to them you will say nothing, make no statements, and ask no questions. Just write it down, talk to your attorney afterward. So then they had to express themselves to you with a lot of barbs on the other side. You allowed them all the freedom in the world to express that, and then told them when they go to the room they would say nothing. Even though you told the defendants they would have to suck it up, they didn't have to because the plaintiffs were instructed not to say a word, and they followed the instructions.

And then you brought them into the room. You invited the defense attorney to do her introduction and run the show. You hardly said a word. The attorney then invited every board member to speak to their assigned subject, and each of them was conciliatory and did remarkably well. The plaintiffs just listened and wrote furiously. They did not say anything. They did not roll their eyes. They were very well behaved. They left. They went back into their own room.

We went back in there with them. We let them download at us, more complaining, not true, this is true, didn't address this, and so on. And this was I thought your most clever moment. You said to them, okay, we didn't address this and this, but everything else is handled. That's what you said to them. Now it wasn't actually true, you know. They hadn't actually come to resolution at that point, but you had come to a resolution and you were convincing both sides that they had. And they went along with you. Every issue was decided kind of by default, except the lawyers' fees, which you never even talked about. But you told both sides that they had handled and agreed upon everything. And you actually said to the other side when we left, write it up.

Soon there was nothing left except who pays the attorney's fees. They already had a deal, though it took a long time to reconcile the two drafts; meanwhile, the negotiation went on over the attorney fees, but they couldn't blow the whole deal over attorney fees, so it got negotiated as we went along. It was getting late. The amount was agreed, the deal was done. What did you do? Both sides felt that you advocated for them. You listened to them vent. They felt very understood, and then they—you know, then you said—basically what they heard was based on what I heard you say, we're settled. That's what they heard and then that's the way they acted for the rest of the day. You let the attorneys hash out the exact semantics of the agreement. And then you had the plaintiffs actually go to the same room with the defendants, shake hands, call it a day.

Elapsed time: 10 hours. We took one 10-minute break.

TENANT vs. LANDLORD

Tenant versus landlord action. This is just the bargaining part.

Plaintiff: This is a no-brainer. $175k.

Defendant: They must be [expletive deleted] joking, offer $5k.

Pl: They don't understand the law. $134k.

Def: This has only nuisance value. $20k.

Pl: We are certain to get an award of attorney fees, which are $75k and counting.

Def: They are liars. Attorney fees cannot exceed $10k.

Mediator: Let's deal with attorney fees separately.

Pl: Okay. $50k plus attorney fees. (At this point, fees not specified.)

Def: No, we won't settle piecemeal. $30k total.

Mediator: Hmm.

Def: $45k is our absolute max.

Mediator: How about $50k? It's an emotional number.

Def: (Thinks deeply.) We will never offer it. But if they demand it, we will accept. Offer good for ten minutes.

Pl: Good grief. Must talk with client privately and call co-counsel.

Mediator: Takes break.

Pl: Okay, $50k.

Def: Okay, $50k.

Elapsed time, 4 hours.

Practice comment: Plaintiff sent no brief in advance but brought a fourteen-page brief to the mediation with a bunch of attachments. This is way too late.

Practice comment: Defendant lawyers showed up with no clients and no adjuster. Plaintiffs were outraged and threatened a bad faith motion, but not after the case settled.

THE WELL-DRESSED DEFENDANT

This defendant was on the hook for some violations as a landlord, and it's just bad luck for him that he will look to the court like a slumlord even though he isn't. He has an attorney who doesn't know the law and hasn't prepared the case. He is against a plaintiff attorney who trawls these waters as a specialty like a shark off a reef, and is well prepared.

Fact is, this was the defendant's very first purchase and he got ripped off by just about everyone including the seller (disappeared) and his realtor/ mortgage broker (filed bankruptcy), so when his tenants came round for yet another bite out of him, he was ready to scream blue murder, which he did to me for quite a while, because his lawyer was late.

The plaintiff lawyer is smart; prepared; and, most important, not greedy, though he starts high.

$50,000	$7,500 (very reluctant)
$42,500	$10,000 (don't have it)
$33,000	$12,000 (they should be paying me)
$28,500	$15,000 (in 90 days)

Defendant says he doesn't have $10,000, much less $12,000, let alone $15,000. He is the aggrieved party here. He knows nothing and is an innocent man. He has a very smooth patter, though he tends to oversell the story.

But he is wearing Prada shoes and a $15,000 watch. If pleading poverty, dress the part.

Plaintiff attorney refuses any delay in payment but still counter demands at $24,000. It is fairly likely that anyone who demands $24k is mentally preparing to land at $20,000. So, we are really discussing a number between $15k and $20k. Even though the gap between them is quite small, the relative incompetence of the defendant's attorney meant that the case did not settle, at least not that day.

A THING GONE WRONG

Terminated employee—no vehicle, unemployed a year, representing self. Wants his job back.

Employer—represented by two human resources (HR) people, both competent, fully documented file. "We are here to listen, but no job, sorry."

Employee—trampled by Fate, concatenation of circumstances, the disaster happened because he trusted a "friend" who betrayed him. It was a great job and being unemployed is no kind of life; he is living practically on air, in fact he has not eaten that day.

Challenge—the HR people are suits, but so am I, even more so. Claimant is not. Will he trust me?

Procedure—claimant gets four-fifths of mediator time. We discuss kids, wife, girlfriend, cars, nutrition, the job, previous jobs, and so on. We discuss what happened. Hard lesson, lousy consequences. He is talking with me, and we are establishing rapport. Ethical issue: what am I going to do with this rapport?

Then the disaster happens—the HR people are chatting in corridor and claimant's buddy allegedly overhears them joking disrespectfully about claimant's mother. The buddy immediately reports this to claimant, who freaks out. Even though the details are not that clear, this is a massive Thing Gone Wrong. The suits are in prompt denial, and I will never get the truth established, but it doesn't matter because claimant will believe his pal no matter what. It's all about perception at this point. He's very upset, and now he really wants to walk out.

Repairing this is very delicate. He wants to leave, so I go with that desire and walk with him into the parking lot, not saying anything but staying close. Fortunately, I spent the previous hour getting to know this man who is terribly upset. We walk around the parking lot, up and down. For a while we are both quiet, then he discusses his stomach, which is churning. He feels terrible but, after we have been walking around for close to thirty minutes, he calms down and decides to stay. I haven't said much at all, just listened to him.

Further repair—I ask HR person to apologize for the upset caused, even though he denies that he said what's alleged. But he agrees to offer an apology, and I am impressed. It's a bit messy, but it definitely does help.

Negotiation—after all this drama, HR mentions a sum of money by way of settlement.

Practical issue—the claimant is not a negotiator, and he didn't come for money, so what to do? As he can't get what he wants, the question is, will he take what he needs?

More to and fro between HR and mediator—a larger sum is mentioned and presented to claimant.

Claimant says, "If you were me, would you take this deal?" I say "Yes," although of course it is up to him to decide, and he could decline. But he agrees to the deal.

Elapsed time: 5 hours

THE VANISHING DEMAND

In this trip-and-fall claim, negotiations went like this:

Plaintiff	Defendant
$400,000	$5,000
$65,000	$7,500
$55,000	$10,000
$15,000	$10,000
$12,500	$10,000
$10,000	$10,000

It seems fantastic that a plaintiff will demand such a large sum and settle for so little. What was the attorney thinking? But he didn't seem to mind falling from the sky in this way.

Negotiation 101: If you start too far out of the ballpark, you sacrifice credibility. There are academic studies that conclude the higher the opening demand, the better the result. This may work in a controlled academic setting, but as real-world advice it is flawed.

Value of claim: The claimant wanted compensation for a fall he sustained on the defendant's premises, claiming he tripped because of a dangerous condition. The problem was that the photographs he produced to show the dangerous condition in fact proved the exact opposite. It simply was not a dangerous condition, an obvious fact shown in the scene photos. But plaintiffs are nothing if not hopeful and sometimes overlook the obvious. The "value" of the claim therefore consists of the defendant's costs of suit plus some multiplier for the extremely outside chance of an upset at trial. This could only be played as a poker game knowing you are not holding any cards.

I feel that had the plaintiff started at $40,000 and come down to around $20,000 and stayed there, there might have been time for the adjuster to make a phone call for some extra money "to put it to bed," and perhaps squeeze a little more money out of the defense. But once you go beyond five p.m., there's no one to call.

Course of mediation: Bulk of time spent with plaintiff. Plaintiff tells story. Look closely at the medicals and discuss them in detail, because that is where their attention is focused. Then discuss causation with attorney, which is where things get sticky for plaintiff. Then discuss liability, which is pretty devastating against plaintiff. Why in this order? Because just as an attorney must establish credibility to be effective in negotiation, so must a mediator be effective in evaluation, and in this situation, the mediator must evaluate at some point. It must be discussed at length so that plaintiff feels fully heard and mediator credibility is established. At that point effective evaluation by the mediator becomes possible. After plaintiff comes down to $55,000, mediator tells plaintiff that his fall could not be due to a dangerous condition because there is no dangerous condition visible in the photograph. It just isn't there, and now really for the first time the obvious is looked at and acknowledged. So demand goes to $15,000 and then down to $10,000.

Why did defendant pay? Because just as corporations don't feel bad when they know they were at fault yet underpay, sometimes they don't feel bad when they were not at fault yet overpay. Corporations have their own logic, and in this case they were willing to pay $10,000 to close their file. So they paid their estimated costs of suit so they could close the file plus, as a sweetener, my fee, which puts more money in plaintiff's pocket. However, this does not always happen.

Elapsed time: 4½ hours

SETTLING FOR NOTHING

This was a limited jurisdiction case, motor vehicle rear-ender, minor alleged injuries, with medical bills around $2,000.

The defense carrier already paid the claimant's property damage. Then they decided not to pay any more. The negotiation went like this:

Demand is $8,500. Defense says no offer.
Plaintiff comes down to $1,000. Defense says no offer.
Plaintiff comes down to $500. Defense says no offer.
Plaintiff demands waiver of costs. Defense says okay.
Case settled.

Elapsed time: 1 hour

Personal injury plaintiff attorneys will sign up cases before knowing the full facts because they cannot know the full facts at the time of getting the retainer signed. So not every case works out, but the client has expectations, and what is the attorney to do other than take a losing case to trial if the defendant refuses to settle?

Here is where an empathetic mediator can be of real help. If the reality of the situation is that this case is a mess and it is economically unfeasible to take it to trial, then it is rational to bite the bullet and move on. Here it helped that the plaintiff got his property damage—his car repairs—paid for. The doctor will have to "eat" the medical bills, but that's okay because he probably gets lots of these types of cases and most pay, so it's a cost of doing business. The attorney will also not recover the filing fee and his other expenses, but that's okay too, because he has other cases and this is a risk of the trade. And the client comes out ahead, because he got medical treatment and car repairs.

The mediator can make it plain to the client in a way that might be awkward for the attorney—that the trial is going to cost money and the client will be on the hook for the defendant's costs if the defendant wins. So the mediator helps the client see the situation for what it is, thus relieving the attorney of this burden. This looks like a dead loss, but really it is the best possible resolution for the plaintiff.

This is exactly the type of case one should be doing pro bono, because if this case is tried, it will cost us taxpayers at least $10,000 just to keep a courtroom occupied and all those government workers filing the paperwork, guarding the doors, and so on, not to mention the productivity loss of all that juror time.

These mediations help both the court and the taxpayer not to have these little cases taking valuable courtroom time.

WRONGFUL DISMISSAL CLAIM OBSERVED BY STUDENT OBSERVER

Mediator: Charles
Apprentice (who wrote this account): Anne
Claimant: James
Respondent: the Electronics Company; its attorney; its investigator; its representative (Michael)

Anne says: In the morning when we arrived I noticed that Charles made an effort to do exactly what he talked about in the class; he offered them coffee, and even though I was there in the position of his assistant he made sure to point out that he was going to get it himself. He got everybody seated in their two rooms. We went in and briefly spoke to the Electronics people and said we were going to talk to James for a while, and we left them alone to talk to James.

We went in and spoke to James for a while—over an hour—and during that time Charles said he was just getting to know James. He showed a lot of empathy for James's position right now. We talked about his family and his children and how his wife was feeling about the whole situation, and so on, and we went back to the Electronics people without really speaking about the case itself at all.

Charles and I had discussed the briefs, and it seemed very open and shut. Certainly we were feeling that way when we walked into the room to the Electronics people. After a little bit of chitchat with the Electronics people we jumped into the case, and everybody sort of nodded at one another and agreed it would be open and shut. They said that they had some money to spend to help him out with certain things, but that it seemed pretty open and closed.

So from there we went back in to speak with James, and everything flipped around very quickly. James's position was that he didn't do any of the things that the investigator had said in the brief, and he was never given a chance to rebut anything that they had said. The investigator asked him a number of questions but in such an informal way that when they ended, the investigator said to James, "You seem like an honest man and we're going to look into this."

James wasn't worried at all, and so when he knew he was being put on suspension pending conclusion of the investigation that seemed fine, but then two weeks later he was given this letter saying that he'd been fired, so he seemed pretty taken aback by the whole process. This was a surprise to me and to Charles, so Charles went through the brief with James piece by piece, having him either confirm or deny each sentence of the investigator's brief.

Then Charles took this information back into the room with the Electronics people. They were extremely surprised and taken aback. The attorney got his blood up and moved into a defensive mode. They all took issue with why James didn't protest more about his innocence during this process. The Electronics attorney got quite heated. He really moved into this mode of total defense and looked very downcast when he thought things were swinging against him, especially when the Electronics representative admitted that they hadn't really given James a chance to tell his side of the story. So then the attorney got the investigator on the phone, and sort of looked at both of us and said, Will you leave us.

When we got back in the room, Charles gets on the phone with the investigator, who says that he had many, "many, many interviews" and admitted that his interview with James had been only 10 or 15 minutes, admitted that he didn't take notes during the interview or have James read or sign any notes. He went through and basically just supported his brief, but in each instance Charles was very careful to go through the brief the same way that he had gone through it with James. In each instance the investigator said well if that's what my report said it must have been right, but admitted that he had absolutely no independent memory of this.

The investigator's dependability on the fact that he was used all the time by the company, that he was trusted, and it was funny because in that conversation the Electronics attorney is saying there's no way he could make a mistake, and he was repeating something back to Charles saying, Well, Charles, you said this and (I can't remember what it was now), but it was something that Charles had not in fact said and Charles said, Well, Mr. Electronics attorney, you just made a mistake right now and we've only been here for five minutes, you've just made a mistake about what I said and you're a very careful person, and I'm not pointing that out to say that that's bad, but just to show how it can happen, it just happened here.

Charles also made the point that when the investigator used quotes for some of James's statements, that some of the things in quotations were in the third person, so clearly they could not have been James's exact words. They had to be through the investigator's perspective, which was I thought a very good point because it meant that the investigator was essentially contradicting his note-taking process. The investigator admitted that he didn't take notes during the interview and that he had written everything down afterward and then built it into a summary.

Charles, who had appeared adversarial while probing in this way, very artfully redirected the entire energy to one of cooperation, saying this was just to show that if I can pick apart this guy in one phone conversation, you're going to have a lot of trouble with him on the witness stand. He repeated he was not advocating for James but only pointing out what might happen if the Electronics company tried to defend, in court, the investigator's manner of investigating. At that point the attorney started to completely soften up, because he was over there, nodding at you, yes, yes, yes, if we take it to court, they'll say this, they'll say that, and then you're talking about the defense people poking holes in what the investigator said, and she really responded to that, and we all had this very frank discussion about what would happen next.

Charles at that point said something that was, I think, a real turning point for them, which was they will look good if they investigate further, because it shows that mediation is meaningful and not just window-dressing. It looks good to be able to say, "We went to mediation. More facts came to light. We reopened the investigation," and if it wasn't true, you reinstated a great employee, but that would really look actually great to employees.

We went back to James and brought him into the other room. They told him all the conditions. He brought up the fact that he would want to talk about money if he was found innocent, to which the Electronics attorney said maybe, but it seemed like that would be very doable, and James brought up the health insurance issue, and the Electronics attorney said she would take care of that. I thought it was actually kind of nice. So James went off and wrote the statement, with some aid from Charles, about how not to get himself into a trap, which I thought was nice, not too much, but some type of how not to get himself into a trap.

We came back and they read the statement, and that was it. Charles made a nice closing statement about the success of the day and just sort of really reframed things nicely, along the lines of there is a man who's saying he's innocent and a company who's really willing to consider that and try to see what was going on, and that's probably the best result that could possibly happen, and I was pretty pleased. I mean, I don't know that James was happy, but I mean, both sides seemed pleased and there were handshakes, so it was good, even for me as your student, who got blamed all day for raising all the devil's advocate questions; no, not blamed, but I did feel the Electronics attorney giving me the stink eye a couple of times across the table.

9. FIVE-CAR PILEUP

This was a five-vehicle rear-end freeway accident—that is, car number one stopped on the freeway and then cars two to five each hit the car in front. This case involved car number three as the claimant against cars four and five, but car four brought a cross-complaint against car two. So we had one plaintiff and three respondents.

I received briefs from all of the respondents, two in advance and one at the start of the mediation. A brief delivered as one walks in the door is of little value compared with one delivered in advance.

But the plaintiff attorney did not provide a brief at all and showed up without his client. What is one to make of this? Does it mean a disinterest in settlement? Not necessarily. All I make of it is that this lawyer is unprepared and expects others to make up for it. Nonetheless, I convened the mediation and commenced by talking with the plaintiff attorney. I had the plaintiff in one room and the three respondents in another room. The best practice is to keep multiple respondents separated, because they tend to reinforce each other's negativity, but it is not always possible.

Everyone agreed that the plaintiff was certain to recover against cars four and five. In other words, this was a clear liability case. The only issue is how much should be paid as compensation.

The plaintiff attorney said his client had $8,000 in medical bills. His demand was for $100,000. From what I had read in the respondents' briefs, the injuries were all soft tissue and had healed. What is the value of this case? It is not my job as mediator to put a value on the case, but it does help to have some idea; I put the range between $15,000 and $30,000, but I kept this to myself.

So how could the plaintiff attorney justify $100,000? It turned out he had not thought about it much. I said it would help if he could provide some justification for the demand, because as soon as I relayed the demand to the respondents, they would ask for it.

The plaintiff attorney then lowered his demand to $65,000. This is a step in the right direction, though it is a bit disheartening when a party lowers a demand by one-third just like that. It suggests that no thought has gone into the bargaining process. But at least I had not communicated the higher demand to the other side. Where is the plaintiff going with this? It is hard to say where he wants to end up. The reason I would not want to communicate such a high demand is that plaintiff attorney would lose credibility and may have to bid against himself, which means the defense refuses to respond at all and the plaintiff must unilaterally lower his demand; this is humiliating, and some plaintiff attorneys will walk out rather that do it.

I presented the demand to the three attorneys for the respondents. One of them gasped and spluttered, and the other two were phlegmatic; in any group of three, someone is always going to provide these kinds of sound effects.

They responded with a combined offer of $7,500. What can one say about this offer? It is low but justifiable as an opening offer against an opening demand of $65,000; I would not have been surprised to hear an opening of $5,000 as a measured response to a demand of $65,000. Where are the respondents going with this? I think they would like to end at $15,000 but are prepared to pay more.

When I presented this offer to plaintiff's attorney, he got up and started to walk out, stating that he had been insulted. I sat him down and asked if he had anything else beyond a soft-tissue injury now recovered. He said his client was still hurting. I asked if he had any medical evidence to back this up. He said his client had told him about it, which is not the same thing.

It will be obvious that the plaintiff attorney is requiring most of the work in this mediation. He had not written a brief. He had not ensured his client's attendance. He pulled dollar numbers out of the air. He felt insulted. He tried to walk out. So we had some talking to do, at the end of which his demand went down to $45,000, and the respondents responded with $12,500.

Next, I spoke on the phone with the client; he told me he was suffering and he was not prepared to be insulted. It is common for dollar numbers to be translated into strong emotional feelings. The difficulty is that most people say they are suffering when they are in a negotiation for compensation. To distinguish one's claim of suffering from everyone else's claim of suffering, one needs corroboration from a doctor. How one feels is a symptom; what the medical tests show is a sign. One needs the symptoms to be correlated with objective medical signs. This case didn't have any such signs.

By this time, plaintiff attorney was ready to bargain for the real value of the case, but his client was not. The client was out of control and, because he was not present at the mediation, it was not possible to get him under control—by which is meant educated to the realities of a system that processes many thousands of similar cases a year.

The plaintiff then came down to $32,000 and the respondents responded with $17,500. I reckoned this case was heading to a settlement of $20,000 to $22,500. Would this have been fair? At $20,000 the attorney would have taken about $7,500 (including costs) and the medicals would have taken another $8,000, leaving the plaintiff with $4,500 (tax free) in his pocket as compensation.

But at this point the plaintiff attorney told me his client had told him to fight the case, so the mediation came to an unsuccessful conclusion.

What happened? The plaintiff attorney was unprepared in numerous ways, but the principal failure was that a meaningful mediation could not occur with the plaintiff because he did not show up. Although the process was effective in changing his attorney's perspective on the case, his client's mind remained unchanged. Even a long phone conversation is ineffective compared with being there. Is this harmful to the client? I think so. Is it possible the client was right about the value of the claim? I do not think so.

In post-mediation follow-up by telephone, the plaintiff attorney reduced his demand to $29,000, but the respondents did not budge from $17,500. A few days later, the plaintiff came down to $25,000. I relayed this demand, and the respondents raised their offer to $20,000, which the plaintiff accepted, and the case settled.

THIRTY TWO

PARTICULAR TYPES OF CASES

INSURANCE CLAIMS

Where an insurance company is involved, the insurance company usually calls the shots provided it can settle the claim within the policy limits in return for a full "Release of all Claims" against its insured. For example, if a motorist is involved in a traffic accident and carries a liability insurance policy with a $100,000 limit, then the insurance company has a duty to defend and, also, the right to settle the case without the consent of the insured for up to the policy limit of $100,000.

If the claim is greater than the policy limits, then the carrier and its insured may be stuck with having to defend against the claim. If the award or verdict is greater than $100,000, the carrier is liable only up to its policy limit, and its insured is "on the hook" for the remainder.

Sometimes a carrier defends against a claim subject to a "reservation of rights" letter. The law makes a distinction between the carrier's "duty to defend," on one hand, and its duty to pay an award, on the other. In such a situation, a carrier may defend its insured against a claim but, if the defense is unsuccessful, leave its insured to pay any award.

Generally, plaintiff attorneys will accept the policy limits, even if the claim is worth more, unless they can be confident of collecting the balance from the insured. Such collection is often difficult, unless the defendant has assets in plain view, such as real estate, that can be seized to satisfy the award.

MEDICAL MALPRACTICE CLAIMS

Medical malpractice insurance policies where a doctor is insured against malpractice liability are an exception, because such policies nearly always require that the doctor give her consent to any settlement. Doctors are reluctant to give consent, because any settlement in excess of a certain amount must be reported to a national registry, so the fact of the malpractice award remains as a permanent item on that doctor's record. The carrier may settle without the doctor's consent if the agreed sum is less than the reportable amount, but most medical malpractice claims carry a higher price tag, making such cases difficult to settle.

Here is an example of one that settled. The patient underwent a surgical operation, during which a small drainage tube was inserted into the wound to assist healing. When the tube was removed some weeks later, a part of it had broken off and was left in the patient's body. However, no difficulties arose for several years, but eventually the plaintiff started to experience pain. For some reason, testing failed to reveal the source of the problem, which was put down to mental stress. That diagnosis caused further distress to the patient. When the existence of the tube was finally discovered in the patient's body and removed, the symptoms promptly ceased. The patient brought a claim against the doctor involved in the original operation and asked for $75,000 in damages. The insurance carrier could offer $30,000, but it could not offer more without the doctor's consent, which he would not give because he did not want a black mark on his record. The mediator suggested that the carrier's representative not bargain—that is to say, not start below $30,000—but immediately put the entire sum on the table, fully explaining the reasons, and pointing out that the carrier would have no option but to proceed to arbitration if the offer was not accepted. The claimant declined the offer because it was so much lower than expectations, but after thinking about it for a couple of days, an immediate $30,000 seemed more attractive than having to go through arbitration, which always carries with it a possibility of either a defense verdict or a damage award less than the $30,000 on offer. So, after a day or two of reflection, the patient accepted.

CONSTRUCTION CLAIMS

Here is an example of negotiation proceeding in numerous baby steps to reach agreement. A married couple complained that the building con- tractor they hired to build them a custom home did it so poorly that rain came in under the door, among numerous other defective items of work- manship. They were angry and upset to find their house appear so poorly constructed. They demanded $89,000 to get all the problems fixed. The defendant offered to pay them $27,000, conceding that although there were clearly some items that needed to be corrected, the plaintiff had greatly exaggerated the extent of the problem. It may be observed that both demand and counteroffer are credible. Even though neither would accept the other's number, the defense offer was not insulting or derisory, such as $5,000 would have seemed, which might have caused the negotiation to end on the spot, and the plaintiff's demand was not outrageous, such as $500,000, which also would have prevented negotiation from occurring. Thereafter, over a period of five hours, the negotiation went through nine stages to arrive at the settlement number, as follows:

Demand(s)	Offer(s)
89,000	27,500
80,000	34,500
72,500	39,500
68,000	43,000
65,000	46,000
62,000	49,000
60,000	52,500
56,000	54,250
55,000	55,000

Mediation theory predicts that settlements will tend to arrive at a point roughly midway between the first credible demand and the first credible offer. According to that theory, this case would settle for $58,250. In fact, it settled for an amount very close to that figure, namely, $55,000. However, there was no way that these particular parties would ever have reached that middle point without going through the intervening steps. This is called the "dance of mediation." Often, impatient parties or their attorneys walk into the room with a demand something like this: "Just tell me your bottom line" or "Let's cut to the chase." This approach would save a great deal of time if it worked—but unfortunately it just does not work. It seems essential that the parties concentrate their attention for a certain period on the problem that they need to solve to summon up the mental energy needed to change from one position to another. They simply cannot make the jump from their expectation to reality in a single jump.

APOLOGIES

Genuine apologies work; fake apologies do not. Any sentence with an "if" in it is fake, as in: "If I hurt you, I'm sorry." For an apology to be genuine, the apologizer has to admit the fault.

In one case, an experienced attorney took on a younger attorney as a partner. Because they knew each other so well, they shook hands on an oral agreement that the younger one would pay the older one in her retirement a percentage of fees brought into the office for a term of years. Such agreements, pertaining to future arrangements, are best made in writing. The younger attorney stopped making payments, resulting in litigation.

Lawyers routinely tell their clients to put such agreements in writing, yet where their own affairs are concerned, they often make the same mistakes that they charge their clients a good deal of money to fix. In this case the two attorneys were represented by lawyers, but for some reason angry hostility developed between the lawyers that was hindering any possibility of settlement. So the mediator took the unusual step of persuading the representing lawyers to leave the room so that the two former partners could confront each other in the presence of the mediator.

The mediator coached the younger attorney to thank the older attorney for all that she had done for her, and to apologize for breaking their oral agreement. It was difficult to persuade the younger attorney to make such an apology and, at first, she wanted to say only: "If I have upset you, I am sorry." This is not an apology. An apology must accept responsibility: "I upset you, I was wrong to do so, I apologize."

The mediator persisted until the younger attorney was willing to accept the obvious, which is that she had indeed upset her former partner, so that she finally got to the point of willingness to make an unreserved and sincere apology, and agreed to make amends for withholding payments. Likewise, faced with a genuine apology, the older attorney immediately softened her attitude, and the two were then easily able to work things out between them.

FAMILY DISPUTES

Family disputes present particular challenges, especially where children are involved. Family disputes can be particularly bitter and vicious. In a dispute involving children, the parents may go to great lengths to defeat the other's interests. Often the paramount interest of the child is overlooked in the struggle for custody.

The courts prefer to endorse arrangements whereby the parents each have the most access possible to the child. The difficulty with these disputes is that in the interests of the child, the parties need to maintain a working relationship until the child reaches the age of maturity, yet the marriage relationship is breaking up often in conditions of bitterness and despair. The legal system has no mechanism for effectively dealing with this problem, which is essentially a problem of human relationships. Many attorneys work with family counselors to help the couple achieve some stability before their split, for the sake of the children.

In addition to the children, a marriage often involves a very involved financial relationship. In this sense, the breakup of a marriage is the breakup of a business partnership, and the question arises how the many assets of the marriage are to be divided and distributed. Family mediations may take many sessions, and it is time well spent if satisfactory conclusions can be reached. One might even say that no one should be allowed to divorce until they have achieved the kind of relation that does not need to break up.

When unmarried couples break up, there is no need for court involvement. One case involved the breakup of the relationship between two women. The end of their relationship was caustic and emotional. There were no children involved, but the couple fought bitterly over every item of property. What turned the process eventually into a kind of reconciliation was the issue of the couple's four cats. One party wanted to bargain for the cats, perhaps distributing them in pairs. The other felt exceedingly emotional about keeping all four cats together. The mediator persuaded the first party to offer the cats, all of them, to the other party entirely without conditions, not as a bargaining chip but as a gesture of goodwill. That small act of kindness so overwhelmed the cat recipient that she was then willing to reciprocate with concessions of her own, and the entire property distribution was soon completed to their mutual satisfaction.

COLLECTIONS CASES

Collections cases are all about the money. The creditor wants to get paid, but the debtor is unwilling or more often unable to pay. These cases are always negotiable, but there is a personal aspect to them as well. The effort of the creditor is to get as much of the total sum owed as possible. Areas of negotiation are as to the amount—that is to say, a discount that the creditor will take to get some of the debt returned—and to payment on terms where the creditor agrees to pay a small but regular amount every month until the debt is paid.

The willingness of creditors to negotiate depends upon whether they believe the debtor has assets that can be seized and whether the debtor has a regular job, because wages can be seized—garnished—by court order. Where the debtor does not have a regular job, which may include many well-paid occupations such as real estate sales agent or professional person working for herself, there is no regular wage check to garnish. It is remarkable how few people own property other than the house they live in, and those family residences are nearly always subject to a large mortgage. All these factors make creditors willing to negotiate.

MEDIATING LEGAL ISSUES

It is next to impossible to mediate a legal issue, because lawyers are trained from their first day at law school to argue legal points and it is generally impossible to get a lawyer to concede a legal argument. That is because laws are composed of language, and language always contains the possibility of ambiguity. Further, it goes against the grain for a lawyer to give up on a legal point, and it is therefore wise for the mediator not to get into a long-drawn-out argument about whose view of the law is correct. The purpose of the mediation is not to decide a point of law, which is the function of judges. Lawyers spend their lives arguing the law before the courts and will argue a point in the way that seems to favor their own side, leaving it up to the judge and sometimes the appeals court to determine the issue.

Therefore, it is often futile to allow mediation to deteriorate into a kind of legal discussion, although it can help lawyers to clarify their thinking. The point of the mediation is to resolve the dispute in a manner in which the parties find mutually satisfactory. Parties never care about the finer points of the law. They simply want to get their dispute resolved without further expense.

DRAWING STRAWS

One can go through an entire career without ever experiencing this, but in one instance the attorney on one side was prepared to draw straws for a huge sum of money. This is not something that a mediator can suggest on her own initiative. In this case, the parties were arguing over a piece of property in which they were partners, and one wanted to buy the other out. The only question was the amount. One party held out for $19 million, the other for $20 million, and there they reached an impasse. The parties asked the mediator to make a proposal, which was then made at $19.6 million.

However, one party declined to accept that proposal. So the attorney for the other side made three "straws" out of strips of paper, writing on them respectively $19 million, $19.5 million, and $20 million. He offered the straws to the other side; the choosing side had a one-third chance of getting the full $20 million and a two-thirds chance of getting either $19.5 or $19 million. The choosing party then elected to take the mediator's proposal, for $19.6 million, that gave them an additional $100,000, so the case was settled on those terms.

CONSUMER CLAIMS (PERSONAL INJURY CASES)

Personal injury case negotiations are generally zero sum in character, meaning whatever one side gains the other side loses. In such cases it is seldom possible to explore underlying interests; this is so for several reasons. The overwhelming majority of personal injury cases are taken on the plaintiff's side on a contingency fee basis, which means that the plaintiff's attorney has no reason to negotiate for anything other than the highest possible amount. The parties are nearly always complete strangers. The only interest the defendant has is in concluding the matter with the least expense possible.

That means that the positions of each side are diametrically opposed, that is to say, if the plaintiff is to receive more, it necessarily follows that the defendant must pay more, and vice versa. So personal injury negotiations are conducted on the basis of calculations involving convenience and assessment of risks. Convenience expresses the idea that personal injury litigation involves more than just money. It also involves stress, time, and missing possibilities, and the conflict consumes not only time but attention—attention that can be put to much better and often more profitable use. This is sometimes called "lost opportunity costs."

This is expressed in a number of colloquial phrases, such as "time to move on" and "putting the matter to bed." It is often worth the plaintiff's while to take a little less, and the defendant's while to pay a little more, just so that they can move on with their lives and to more profitable pursuits. The second factor is calculation of risk, because of the uncertainty of a better outcome in a trial. Some people are sophisticated in their estimation of risk, whereas others do it fairly unconsciously. But in calculating an acceptable settlement amount, everyone takes into consideration the possibility of doing worse at trial.

This is so ubiquitous that it has its own acronym: BATNA, meaning Best Alternative to a Negotiated Agreement. This is also known as WATNA, meaning Worst Alternative to a Negotiated Agreement. These acronyms invite the negotiator to consider the future and ask, "If I do not settle today, what is likely to happen down the road? Could I get a better outcome, or may things get worse?"

To avoid the uncertainty of a worse outcome, the plaintiff may take a little less and the defendant may pay a little more. The difference between the plaintiff's idea of what a case is worth and the amount the plaintiff is willing to accept may be called the *premium*. The defendant pays more than its evaluation of the case value, and this also can be considered as a premium. It is sometimes said that a settlement is satisfactory if both sides are unhappy with the result. However, although buyer's remorse and seller's remorse is not uncommon, within a day or two it is generally the case that both sides are glad that it is over.

Think about it carefully! Don't go off somewhere else!
...throw away all thoughts of imaginary things
And stand firm in that which you are.

—Kabir, 1440-1518

APPENDIX

Checklist for mediators

Convening

1. Agree on a date, time, place, fees, number of participants, and ground rules.
2. Send letter to parties confirming these arrangements.

Opening

3. Introduce yourself and the parties.
4. Ask for the job of mediator in this dispute and obtain consent.
5. Ask for agreement on ground rules, that is, civil behavior.

Communicating

6. Commence communication, either jointly or privately or both.
7. Stay focused on the problem that must be resolved.
8. Keep the conversation going and the channels of communication open.

Negotiating

9. Narrow the areas of disagreement.

10. Keep moving in the direction of more agreement.

11. Get to the ZOPA.

Closure

12. Narrow the distance between the parties to zero.

13. Acknowledge the moment of closure.

14. Write it up and get signatures. Thank the participants.

A Lawyer's Checklist For Mediators

Introduction

1. Forget formality and opening statements.

2. Brief introduction and get confidentiality signed.

3. It is the attorneys' job to handle their clients.

4. Candy and snacks do not help much.

5. Yours is a supporting role; leave your ego behind.

Approach

1. Know the type of case, as the approach will vary (e.g., medical malpractice, business dispute).

2. Know the attorneys (trial attorney vs. inexperienced attorney).

3. Shuttle diplomacy works.

4. Show you care; earn trust and confidence.

What to Avoid

1. Avoid arbitrary figures and preset settlement goals.

2. Avoid dwelling on weaknesses or harsh criticisms.

3. Avoid putting warring parties/attorneys together.

4. Do not be deterred by posturing and pronouncements of "rock bottom" and "not one penny" offers.

5. Avoid giving up too quick. Keep at it.

Common Problems

1. Lack of authority or consent; lack of client control.

2. Lack of access to adjuster or home office.

3. Lack of knowledge about the case.

4. Lack of civility between lawyers.

What Works

1. Ask what you can do.

2. Offer alternatives and ideas.

3. Be nice, positive, and flexible.

Conclusion

1. Offer follow-up sessions when timing may be better.

2. Make follow-up calls to check on status.

3. The art of making settlements requires patience, compassion, listening skills, and good luck.

*Thanks to Los Angeles attorney David Drexler for permission to use this Lawyer's Checklist.

Alternative Checklist For Mediators

Phase 1: Introduction

____ Names of everyone present
____ Ground rules, confidentiality
____ Explanation of mediation

Phase 2: Telling the Story

____ Listen
____ Paraphrase or reframe (as needed)
____ Acknowledge

Phase 3: Understanding the Problem

____ Listen for issues
____ Listen for needs
____ Point out areas of agreement
____ Brainstorm

Phase 4: Resolution

____ Evaluate ideas one at a time
____ Consider workability
____ Make sure agreements are specific
____ Make sure agreements are balanced
____ All parties to sign

Self Evaluation Form

1. Communicate clearly and effectively to the disputants.

2. Demonstrate impartiality while maintaining control of the process.

3. Maintain poise.

4. Avoid annoying mannerisms.

5. Make a professional impression.

6. Show sensitivity to the reactions and feelings of others.

7. Respond appropriately and effectively.

8. Exhibit ease and vigor in approaching a new situation.

9. Carry discussions to completion.

10. Hold determined intention to help parties achieve results.

11. Express thoughts in a clear, unbiased fashion.

SELECT READING LIST

Against the Gods, Peter L. Bernstein (1996, 1998)
The 48 Laws of Power, Robert Greene (1998)
The Art of Seduction, Robert Greene (2001)
Bad Boys, Bad Men, Donald W. Black (1999)
Bad Men Do What Good Men Dream, Robert I. Simon (1996)
Bargaining for Advantage, G. Richard Shell (1999)
The Blank Slate, Steven Pinker (2002)
Blink: The Power of Thinking Without Thinking, Malcolm Gladwell (2005)
Beyond Reason: Using Emotions as You Negotiate, Roger Fisher and Daniel Shapiro (2005)
Changing Minds, Howard Gardner (2004)
Conflict Mediation Across Cultures, David W. Augsberger (1992)
Conquering Deception, Jef Nance (2000)
The Corporation, Joel Bakan (2002)
The Crossroads of Conflict, Kenneth Cloke (2010)
The Death of Common Sense: How Law Is Suffocating America - Philip K. Howard (1995)
The Dynamics of Conflict Resolution: A Practitioner's Guide, Bernard Mayer (2000)
Emotional Intelligence: Why It Can Matter More Than IQ, Daniel Goleman (2006)
Gangs of America, Ted Nace (2003)
Getting Past No, William Ury (1993)
Getting to Yes, Roger Fisher and William L. Ury(1981)
Influence: The Power of Persuasion, Robert B. Cialdini (2001)
Inside the Criminal Mind, Stanton E. Simenow (1984/2004)

Intuition at Work, Gary Klein (2002)

Lying: Moral Choices in Public and Private Life, Sissela Bok (1978)

Mediation, Jay Folberg and Alison Taylor (1984)

Mediating Dangerously, Kenneth Cloke (2001)

Mediation: A Psychological Insight Into Conflict Resolution, Freddie Strasser (2004)

Mediation Process, Christopher W. Moore (1986/2003)

Mediation Field Guide, Barbara Ashley Phillips (2001)

Mediation Theory and Practice, Suzanne McCorkle and Melanie J. Reese (2005)

Negotiating Rationally, Max H. Bazerman and Margaret Neale (1992)

Never Be Lied to Again, David J. Lieberman (1998)

Nonviolent Communication: A Language of Life, Marshall B. Rosenberg (2003)

The Origins of Virtue, Matt Ridley (1996)

Secrets of Power Negotiating, Roger Dawson (2001)

Secrets: On the Ethics of Concealment and Revelation, Sissela Bok (1983)

The Social Structure of Right and Wrong, Donald Black (1993)

The Sociopath Next Door, Martha Stout (2005)

Sources of Power: How People Make Decisions, Gary Klein (1998)

Speak Peace in a World of Conflict, Marshall B. Rosenberg (2005)

Start with NO, Jim Camp (2002)

The Winner's Curse, Richard H. Thaler (1994)

Without Conscience, Robert D. Hare (1993)

ENDNOTES

1. Kenneth Cloke, *Mediating Dangerously: The Frontiers of Conflict Resolution* (San Francisco, CA: Jossey-Bass, 2001).

2. Bernard S. Mayer, *Beyond Neutrality: Confronting the Crisis in Conflict Resolution* (San Francisco, CA: Jossey-Bass, 2004).

3. Erwin Schrodinger, *Schrodinger's Science and the Human Temperament* (New York: Norton, 1935).

4. Richard Phillips Feynman, *The Feynman Lectures on Physics* (Boston: Addison-Wesley, 1966).

5. George Barker, "True Confession," 1950.

6. George Steiner, *Antigones* (Oxford, UK: Clarendon, 1984).

7. Ibid.

8. Ibid.

9. John Donne quote (1631).

10. Niall Ferguson, *Empire: How Britain Made the Modern World* (New York: Penguin, 2004).

11. See www.medterms.com (Retrieved June 24, 2019).

12. Jim Britt, *Freedom: Letting Go of Anxiety and Fear of the Unknown* (Mesa, AZ: Dandelion Books, 2003).

13. Christopher W. Moore, *The Mediation Process: Practical Strategies for Resolving Conflict* (San Francisco, CA: Jossey-Bass, 2014).

14. Howard Gardner, *Changing Minds: The Art and Science of Changing Our Own and Other People's Minds* (Cambridge, MA: Harvard Business Review Press, 2006).

INDEX

conflicts
 defense of, 37–39
 derivative conflict, 14
 disputes versus, 33
 factors distinguishing, 145–147
 five orders of, 43–45
 nature of, 33–36, 42–43
 necessary conflict, 41–45
 unwillingness to give up, 112–113
 wrong targets in, 21–22
confrontation strategy, 19–20
Confucius, 54
consensus, 162
consistencies, 153–154, 162
construction claims, 211–212
consumer claims (personal injury cases), 216–217
contract negotiations, 153
convenience, 216
convening stage of negotiation, 109–110
cooperation, 10, 39, 185, 187–188. *See also* prisoner's dilemma
Copernican mediocrity principle, 170–171
cost/reward analysis, 168
courage, 54
courtesy, 61
credibility, 198–199
credible zone, 12, 130, 212
crying, 94–95
cultural awareness, 69–70

dance of mediation, 212
data-gathering process, 144
debt collection cases, 214
deception, 151–155. *See also* lies, clues about
decisiveness, 53, 115
defection, 181. *See also* prisoner's dilemma
demands/offers, 12–13, 128–129, 205
de minimis phenomenon, 157–158
denial stage of grief, 157–158
depression stage of grief, 159
De Profundis (Wilde), 116
derivative conflict, 14
desires versus wounds, 34, 35, 127–128
dictators, 141–142
diplomacy, war versus, 28
disentanglement, 55, 160
disputes, 33, 102–104, 114–115. *See also* vignettes; *specific types of disputes*
distraction, 48
distributive bargaining, 126
divorce, collaborative law and, 21
doubt, certainty and, 149–155
drawing straws, 173, 215
duty to defend versus duty to pay, 209
dynamics of mediated negotiation, 99–106

Earhart, Amelia, 54
Einstein, Albert, 89

ACKNOWLEDGEMENTS

An acknowledgement is like a guest list, always a delicate matter because one can never be inclusive. As soon as I started to write this acknowledgement I realized that more people have helped me than I have space to name or brain to remember. As a little boy, my mama and aunties read to me, when the men were all away at war. Only much later did I realize what a great gift it was.

At my primary school, Mrs. Flynn the headmaster's wife twisted my ear, benignly, to get me into the habit of reading for myself. When I was eleven and about to depart to Australia, Mr. Horn the English teacher provided words of encouragement. I expect he immediately forgot those words, but I did not. So many others have done much the same for me.

When I was getting into mediation, after many years of law practice, Natalie Armstrong and Andrew Golden afforded me the opportunity to teach at the Institute for Conflict Management in Los Angeles (ICM), which was invaluable to me, as it complemented my own experience as a lawyer, arbitrator, part-time judge, and mediator. At ICM I put in nearly a thousand hours, much of it with fellow attorney Robert Tessier, which proved that the best way to learn is to teach.

My wife Charlotte, who publishes under the name Charlotte Laws, has been indispensable helping to put this book together. I would say to the rest "you know who you are," except that really they don't and neither do I. A complete list of people I am grateful for would be close to an autobiography, as I have the sense of being held in a web of influencers, bound with a common thread of appreciation

I dedicate this book to my 11-year-old grandchild Scarlett, who as well as being an accomplished dancer has already read a million words and is well into her second. Dancing is her passion, reading an investment in forever.

Printed in Great Britain
by Amazon